Married

to

MARIJUANA

MY LOVE AFFAIR

with

WEED & HIP HOP

by

DJ JASON 'BIG KUSH' BERRY

MARRIED TO MARIJUANA
Published 2017 in U.S.A by Genre/Over The Edge Books

ISBN - 978-1-944082-36-9

Layout by Michael Ziobrowski / @XIsTheWeapon

overtheedgebooks.com

CONTENTS

Married to Marijuana

Hip Hops love affair with Weed Seen Through the Eyes of Big Kush Jay

Chapter 1

It was a hot summer night in LA. The Eminem Anger Management tour had just ended and I was taking some much-needed time with my family. I got a call from the Shady Records VP, it seems the crew was also in town to finish mixing some records with Dre. Having only met the big homie once before at the recent 50 Cent "In the Club" video shoot, I was of course looking forward to the opportunity to link with him again. This particular night Dre was mixing some Obie Trice records and since I had just spent the past 6 weeks with dude, I was invited to baby sit accompany him in the studio for the session. My role at Shady allowed me to wear many hats. Marc, the Shady VP was usually responsible for making sure the sessions ran smoothly, he was also on the tour and was also in need of some R&R. As he ran point, I wanted to continue to prove myself in all capacities. I prepped for the session by calling my cousin Rocbotm from the sixties who usually connected me with the streets of LA. We needed the finest herb Cali had to offer! We was going to smoke with the good doc and I wanted to represent! The year was 2003, and I was still copping my weed from the streets. The uniform was white airs, 501s, and a crisp white tee. During that time, I pretty much wore the same thing every day. Accompanied by a diamond studded big face watch. I never was much into chains and rings, but I love watches. I got a bunch! We hopped in the SuperSport and was off to the Valley. Dre's studio was very inconspicuous, almost hidden. We pulled up to the gated door and got access. The gate opens to reveal a smorgasbord of 600 Benz's, Porches, and Bentleys. The homies ride was clean and gangstad out, still giving us some status in the lot. Greeted by Shady security and others as we were escorted into the control room, where we met with Dre and Obie already hard at work.

This would be my second time meeting Dre. Having worked with and around many artist, there wasn't too many who didn't get me kitty like a school girl. Being a fan of the music and culture first and foremost, I always get excited and get them butterflies when meeting a legend in the game. RocB a South Central native and rapper himself, I could only imagine how he was feeling on the inside. Actually having the opportunity to see the good doctor work and witness the creative process was like having died and gone to rap heaven. Upon entering the studio I was a little apprehensive, anytime an outsider is brought around the label execs and artists you never know how things are going to turn out. Not that I was worried about Rocs actions, but more so about the artists and execs. Keeping the artists 100% comfortable and not interrupting the music process is the priority. I've been in the studio with artists sometimes and seen them kick out people who they felt were disturbing their chi, lol. Our experience was quite the contrary. Producer Mel man promptly walked into the studio with a fat sac and it was on from there. Mel man rolled up, Roc B rolled up, Obie was rappin, Dre was on the boards, and I was in heaven. Obie the consummate drinker and non-smoker was on that brown. Henny seemed to flow from the faucets in the studio, I felt like I was in a video.

Watching Dre meticulously turn the knobs, fuck with the bass, adding sounds and ambiance gave me a new respect for the music I grew up to listening to in my stolen Walkman. While he worked he catered to everyone in the room like a true host. The way we was interacting I felt as if he thought I was someone he had met before. He was so cool to me; I convinced myself he must think I'm someone else. But then I realized that's how dude is, Andre from Compton. His experience and wisdom lit up the room with stories from the Death Row years and musical gems. Sippin on yac and smoking blunts gave him a man of the people kind of feel to me. Even though he was a king in my eyes, he made everyone feel on the same level. As the night progressed, Busta and Spliff Star stopped by to lay his verse for some remix. Already having a relationship with Busta and Spliff from the NYC mix tape scene, the party got even more turntd. As I sat an absorbed the whole scene, I would think to myself as I would often do "I'm from the Roc, I ain't even supposed to be here…"

When I refer to the Roc, I'm talking about my hometown of Rochester, NY. Growing up I often thought of Rochester as the lost city. No one outside of the city, to me at least, had ever heard of it. I never saw it on a TV show, heard about it in a song, never made the national news, nothing. Buffalo had the Bills, Syracuse had SU for notoriety, Albany was the capitol and NYC was the hub of everything in the world. All we had was Kodak and Bausch & Lomb eye wear. Which are both gone now, from the city and existence. Rochester and upstate NY had once been a hub for slaves to escape via the Underground Railroad. We would learn about Frederick Douglass and Harriet Tubman in school. I went to Fredrick Douglas Jr High; we sang songs about dude and everything. For an area that once was a beacon of hope for people of color seems to be an area now filled with disparity now for myself and other people of color.

My Mom was from the backwoods of Poughsville, Va. A small town near Norfolk. Just imagine the Color Purple and that was Poughsville. When I was a kid my Mom and her sisters would watch that movie over and over. I didn't realize at the time, but it was filled with reminders of home. My Dad is from Rochester, via West Va, where my Grandfather was from. Cole mining runs in my blood. They met via a mutual friend. Much of my childhood is a blur. My Mom and I moved to Washington D.C. briefly during my childhood after their divorce. I remember us moving back to Rochester to live with my Dad during the reconciling years. This is when I was first introduced to weed! I was around the age of 8 by now. My younger brother Michael had been born, and we moved to a bigger home on Bowman St. near East High. It seems my pops had picked up some habits while away from my Mom. Or maybe he had had them all along, and during their separation these habits had become more prevalent. It wasn't the sort of thing he would do in front of me of course, but me as a very precocious kids, I was into everything. I remember him having a bong/water pipe that resembled an Indian Peace Pipe. When I saw him hit it, I asked him what it was, and that's what he said. He told me he used it to stay at peace. Of course, I was confused at the time, but fascinated by the concept of blowing a peace pipe to maintain the peace, it made perfect since to me. Not to mention, the lovely fragrance. I loved the smell of weed burning, anytime as a kid I would smell it, I would automatically gravitate toward it. Back in the day pops would burn some incense to mask the smell, but I knew what time it was. When asking my Dad can I hit the peace pipe, he told me you are already at peace, so there's no need. "You have no worries, in due time son" is what he would tell me. Regardless of what he told me, I couldn't wait till I was old enough to hit the peace pipe. The imagery of him breaking up some bud, tightly packing the bowl, taking a snap, seeing the smoke form in the bowl area, and then disappears. Only to reappear in my father lungs and then to eventually come out of his mouth and nose was like a cool ritual I wanted to reenact for myself. I thought it was part of the calming process, like saying "Hooossaaa" while meditating and contorting your fingers and hands in a certain way, lol. The only other person close to me who I had ever seen around weed was my Uncle Earl! My Uncle Earl is my Mom's youngest sibling, the baby of the family. My favorite Uncle! He was the youngest adult in the family, so of course that made him the coolest. He would roll joints on Parliament Funkadelic and Rick James album covers. While the music played he would smoked his spliff, I would read the funny comics and liner notes on the back of the albums.

We only lived with my pops for a short period of time before it was just me Mom and my brother once again alone to fend for ourselves. My pops paid child support every month, but it was never enough. So saying we were broke was an understatement. My Mom kept a full time job, but the term "robbing Peter to pay Paul" was said very often. We never got food stamps, but I'm sure we could've used them. She always made sure we had clothes on our backs and food in our mouths, how she did it was the question. Name brands never made into my house. Some people had Cheerios; we had "Bowls of Os". Others had Sergio Valente and Guess Jeans stone wash jeans. I would have to wear the same 2nd hand store jeans until the space where my thighs would rub together completely faded away. For most of my middle school years I had to sit with my legs closed, just to not get picked on by bullies looking to further their popularity. By High School I had a job and was able to buy my own school clothes, thank god! By High School my focus was purely on finding a way out! I was smart, and school came pretty easy. I was taking a bunch of Science and Technology courses. I went to Wilson Magnet HS, one of the best High Schools in the city. I graduated with a 2.95 GPA just short of Honor roll for the year. My Mom wanted me to become an engineer, in the hopes that field would give me job stability and affluence. I decided to go with my main Love, HIP HOP! I was your typical kid with rap posters all over my walls. Big Daddy Kane, KRS-1, Heavy D, and many others, these were the people I would tell my dreams to at night. I never wanted to be a rapper or a DJ; I wanted to be the businessman. I wanted to be Russell Simmons. Russell was the mastermind behind many of raps early artists. Not just Run-DMC, but Kurtis Blow, EPMD and many others. He had a management team called RUSH. That's what they called him. "Rollin wit RUSH" if you were signed to him, you were "Rollin wit RUSH!" I would read Word Up, The Source and many other rap rags at the time to get my information. My Mother would always instill in me that I was special, and that I could do anything that I put my mind to. Of course since we didn't have a lot of money, my family was over flowing with Love. Although sometimes, I often wished we just had the money. Later in life when I had the opportunity to work with Russell, I would call him RUSH. Made me feel like I knew him when he was called that. I wish I had a smoking with Rush story, but unfortunately he was clean by the time I met him. But Green and I would smoke out his Maybach often while waiting on him to get out of Yoga. Sometimes that would be the best way to meet with him. Ambushing him in a cloud of smoke after he just worked out. I know he just tolerated us because we was signed to him, but I knew he hated that shit. But his driver and long time homie would let us in while we waited. What else was we supposed to do. Smoke out the Maybach!

By the time I was 13, my Dad had remarried to a woman named Gayle, who had a son 3 yrs. older than I, named Lamont. Well his name is Michael, but we all called him Lamont. It took a while for Lamont and I to get along. Not only was it a shock to me that my pops was getting remarried, but now I must share him with his new wife and her 16 yr. old son, I felt as if I was being replaced. To ease the relations and to help develop the friendship I often stayed with my Dad over the weekends, some Holidays, school vacations, etc. I think it was just as much of a disturbance for him as it was for me. By this time, my Dad was a devout Christian and a member of the Church of Christ. Which pretty much means I became a member of the Church of Christ. It was pretty cool, much of my family had converted to this Church, and so we often saw each other on Sundays. To this day my family are members of this same church.

Lamont and I after our probationary period for each other found each other to be very cool. We are still very good friends to this day. Of course him being an older big brother figure for me was great. He introduced me to many great things besides weed. He opened my eyes to a lot of other music I probably wouldn't have listened to if it wasn't for him. Bands like the Police, Genesis, Pink Floyd, The Time and a bunch of Prince shit. He hung around a lot of White guys growing up. Black guys too, but he def had a White boy crew. He was the first person I knew to seemlessly move in both circles with out compromising who he was. They would kick it in the cemetery, smoke weed and drink 40's, kid shit. This was the 80's; Black and White relations were nowhere near where they are now. I had my first weed experience with Lamont. We went to the same High School. As I was a Freshman entering into Wilson, he was a senior on his way out the door. This was the summer before Freshman year. Lamont was preparing to go to the movies with some friends. I guess My Dad and Gayle wanted the house to themselves so they insisted he take me. With some slight resistance, it was on! I didn't know what to expect. I had never been out of the house in this capacity without parental supervision. As soon as his homies pulled up the debauchery began. With Lamont and me the car was 5 deep. First stop to the store that sells beer to minors. We pooled our resources and purchased 40oz's of Old English malt liquor, one for everybody. Now off to the movie theatres. I'm sitting in the backseat, the music is stoopid loud. I can't even make out the words. I'm trying to chug my 40 to prove I wasn't no punk. I was having too much fun; I didn't want to give the guys any chance to turn me down for the next trip. Nightmare on Elm St was the flick. I was kinda scared, but couldn't show any fear with the older guys. On our way to the movies, I smelled that glorious aroma I was so familiar with as a kid. There was a joint going around, I was so excited I was gonna actually have the chance to hit it! They asked me had I ever smoked, of course I said no. They gave me the rules. Take a puff and hold it in and then exhale. I was told it might burn a little bit, and not to take more than 2 puffs. I was also told I would be kicked out the car if I got the joint all wet. I took a hit; it tasted like nothing I had ever tasted. Def harsh though. I'm sure it was probably full of seeds, sticks and stems but we was getting high! By the time we arrived to the movie theatre, I was told not to be acting all crazy to not alert the adults in the theatre to our inebriation. I had never felt like that before. It felt as if I was floating in the theatre. My eyes were super glassy and my paranoia level was on 100! After ordering loads of popcorn and candy we bum rushed the show. I was so freaked out, but couldn't let on of course. Just thinking of Freddy Krueger coming to get me in my dreams, all while high for my first time, TRIPPPPYYY!! After we left the theatre we smoked some more, finished our flat 40s, and hit up the cemetery. All of this after seeing Nightmare on Elm St. The cemetery was pretty much a place unpoliced at night, so it was the perfect area to go kick it, just as long as you weren't scared. I first thought we were hittin up the cemetery to further freak me out, but then I realized this was part of the regular antics of the crew. After smoking, drinking, and 1,000 jokes later we finally went home. Not that I wasn't enjoying myself anymore, but I was extremely tired. I wasn't used to staying up that late yet. A skill I had to mature into. Now that I was finally home and in my bed, I was too scared to go to sleep with the fear that Freddy was going to come and get me, lol.

I would only smoke with my brother and his crew at the time. Fall came and by the time I got to High School, all of his friends already knew of me as the little homie that could hold his own, giving me instant respect with the older heads. Lamont would steal weed out of his pops or his uncles stash and we would smoke every once in a while when available. Still very far and few in between the times we would smoke.

By College, I still wasn't much of a weed head. Probably due to the fact that I couldn't readily find it and my homies at the time wasn't into it. But at a party, if I smelt it, I wasn't far from it. The rap music and the hip hop culture played a major role in my upbringing. By this time, it was the 90's. Weed was the 3rd member of most hip-hop groups at the time. Even though I was a Computer Science major, engineering was the furthest thing from my mind. I had just gotten a beautiful skinny girlfriend, which was a first for me. As I was close to 300 lbs. by my Freshman year in college, the majority of my girl friends up until that time was what we called chunky but funkies. I guess that's why I fell so hard for her. The party scene was where I lived the majority of my Freshman year. I was having sex and partying every other night, there was no stopping me. Oh I guess there was some stopping, by the end of Freshman year Buffalo State had had enough of my shenanigans and kicked me out of school; back home to my mommas house I went. I enrolled in the community college, MCC tucked my tail and started Freshman year over. This time with a little bit more focus, I was voted the vice president of The Association of the African American Students (T.A.A.A.S) Through my role as VP I learned much about school politics and bullshit. But mostly I learned, that if you're on the executive board of school group, you have access to the budget. The larger the group the larger the budget. We were pretty large. With at least 2 signatures from the Exec board and a group's counselor signature, a check could be cut. Most of our counselors were pretty strict, but there was always one that was cool. Once becoming familiar with the process, we were getting checks cut all day! We didn't steal per say, just did a little creative budgeting, I would say. Administration fees we called it. The American way! One of the other members on the E board was my man DJ Big Reg! Who introduced me to DJ Green Lantern. My first 2 DJ's I ever managed and worked with. They had a radio show on the local college radio station WITR that broadcasted from Rochester Institute of Technology, RIT. College Radio was the only place in the

90's to hear real rap music spun by real hip-hop DJs. We represented that for our area at that time. The only place where you was going to hear Brand Nubian, Diggin in the Crates crew, ATCQ, De La, all that!! That was what we also represented when we spun at parties. We ran the upstate party scene. After a while we played every major club and college in the upstate area. After polishing my check hustling days at MCC, I took my criminal knowledge elsewhere to make money. I would approach other organizations, frats, other school groups, etc. to follow my instructions. I would basically tell the person I was doing the deal with, "if you get the check cut for this amount, I'll kick you down a piece." I would tell the person who was doing the deal, how to get the check cut for a larger amount than what's needed. I would give them their cut, keep my skim, pay everybody, and everybody left happy! I ran this hustle throughout all of the schools in NY state that booked us for a show.

Looking to break out of the upstate local arena, I was itching to make a move to NYC. Hip-hop started in the Bronx and thrived in NYC. All the labels was in NYC. I knew if I was going to make it in the hip-hop scene I had to make a move. Looking to further the careers of the DJ's I was working at the time, I finally got to NYC via my girlfriend at the time. Her mom was an opera singer. She got a gig singing in Germany for a summer, so my girl and I moved into her Harlem studio apartment for the summer. I was in heaven. As a kid I would watch tv shows, movies, read books, anything just to get familiar with the texture of the city. Shows like Barney Miller, The Jeffersons, and Coming to America would stay on repeat in my VCR. I would memorize the names of the buildings and signs just to be familiar with NYC brands and street names. You didn't know NY if you didn't know about Greys Papaya or Katz Deli. Now I finally was there. Now I knew from actual experience that its pronounced, "House ton" not Houston like the city. I learned that Boars Head is the best deli meat for your sandwich. The little things that make you feel like a real New Yorker. I would ride through times square until I ran out of gas just dreaming about running the city one day. My first job in the music industry was an internship at Jive records. Lasted about 2 weeks. I got kicked out because I kept flirting with my boss, who was a young cute, executive who didn't have time for my games. In the Promotions Dept theres always music playing, joking around, etc. It was easy for me to get caught up. Once I got my second job at the Fridge Magazine, I took it much more serious. The Fridge Magazine was an urban skate and snowboarder mag that covered the collision of skate and urban culture. At the time, they needed some "URBAN". I was able to fill the order, and found a home with them. My mentor and still good friend, Jonathan Levine, ran the Fridge. He taught me a lot on how to run a business, and how to hustle the system. He also taught me a lot about weed. It was a small group, the music supervisor, Seth Zaplin aka Seth Dawg, was my partner in crime. We would converse for days over the latest hip-hop scandals and what content would be appropriate for the magazine. Now that I was there, part of my job was to make sure the credibility of the magazine was respected. I was apprehensive initially about taking the job. I wanted to work at a prominent record label, like Bad Boy or Def Jam. But these were the cards I was dealt, so I was determined to make it the best it could be. For an independent magazine, we caused a lot of stir with our interviews, events, parties, and covers. It was all about combining the cultures. We were the first to do skate jams where they played hip-hop and booked rap acts. We would bring hip-hop artists to the tops of mountains for snowboard concerts. We were early consultants for the X Games and the Dew Games produced by Pepsi. We were skate and Snow before it was cool. At these events and while conversing with NYC's hip-hop elite, I became a solidified member of the cannabis culture.

Chapter 2
In my DNA

My Dad is a huge Jazz fan. He travels all over to see various bands at the festivals. As a kid, all I could remember was my Dad with some headphones on looking at the back of some cool Jazz album cover. He would play different tunes for me and break down the instruments and who was playing what. He would explain to me how each player got a chance to get theirs off, and then come back to the hook in a sense. One of our favorite grooves is the classic Chuck Mangione "Feel so Good" I could remember thinking to myself, that's a white dude playing like that?? My Dad would say, "Yea some of the best horn players are white" I would think Jazz must be pretty cool if whites and blacks can play in the same band and make great music!

Marijuana and Jazz music have quite the history. In 1909 the first use of the word "marihuana" was recorded in American music. Storyville, the red light district of New Orleans, deep in the bordellos, is where Jazz music provided the backdrop for the seediest part of town. Weed enabled the musicians to play long and hard sets, helping them to forget their fatigue. Moreover, the weed seemed to make the music sound even more captivating and fresh, especially if you were high while listening.

In the early 1920's weed was commonly referred to as muggles, tea, Mary Jane or Mary Warner, reefers, muta, or sometimes gage. Weed seemed to only exist within this New Orleans sub culture. Many Jazz musicians also sold weed at this time, as a means of extra income. This didn't sit well of course with the white authorities. They expressed that the Jazz music was spreading a powerful new "voodoo" and that the weed they sold made decent folks abandon their inhibitions.

Louis Armstrong born was born in 1901 in New Orleans; he grew up in this environment. The year before his death in 1971, Satchmo collaborated with his biographers Max Jones and John Chilton by sending them recorded audiotapes of him telling his Viper stories. Viper because of the hissing sound made while hitting a joint. A Viper can be from any walk of life, as long as they respect the ganja. "We always looked at pot as a sort of medicine, a cheap drunk and with much better thoughts than one that's full of liquor." Says Louis. In 1931, in between playing a set at the Culver City, Cotton Club, Satchmo was blazing a joint and got arrested. Snitched on by a rival band member, he spent 9 nights in Los Angeles city jail. Facing a 6-month sentence, luckily the judge was a fan and dropped the charges. He went to work to blow his horn that night as if nothing had ever happened. He said the funniest thing about the whole situation was after his set, several movie stars approached him saying they had heard he had got caught with "Mari Huana" aka Mary Warner thinking it was a chic. I'm sure he had wished it was a chic, lol.

My Dad always told me Jazz music was the hip-hop of his generation. Imagine Louis Armstrong, Dizzie Gilespie, and the crew smoking a fat joint before a set. All you would hear is a bunch of hissing in the corner of some Jazzy smokey basement. Reminds me of hip hop in the early 90's when I really first started really partaking in the party life and got formally introduced to smoking fat Philly blunts full of dirt weed, snap crackling, and popping from all the stem, sticks and seeds, lol.

It takes two! Any drug deal there's the buyer and the seller. Jews and Blacks historically have always worked together. This is no different. Milton "Mezz" Mezzrow was a Jewish kid from Chicago. He would kick it with the Black musicians that would hang out at the reformatory where he was determined to become "Negro". First he learned how to play the horn and then he was getting high with the band. By the end of Prohibition, Mezz moved to the capitol city of Black America, Harlem. He had sharpened his sword by playing in the Chicago Speakeasies, and was ready to play with in the big leagues. Upon arrival, he found the weed to be sub par. He also found out he needed a little bit more practice to keep up with the local talent. In an attempt to gain favor with the Brothers, he brought in a strong Mexican weed that had everybody on tilt. Giving him the pass he desperately was seeking. Before long Mezz was the man! All good weed in Harlem was called "Mezz" at that time, he had it on lock! The Branson of his day. He served many of Harlem World's greatest Jazz musicians but his homie Fats Waller was the only one to put him in a song. On "If you're a Viper" Fats raps "Dreamed about a reefer five foot long, might Mezz but not too strong, you'll be high, but not for long, if you're a Viper."

Mezzrow, the horn player he was, got down on a track called "Sendin the Vipers". His musical career is nothing compared to his autobiography "Really the Blues", where he recounts his life with the world's most talented Jazz musicians.

I find it very interesting that one of the most prolific people to shape 90's militant hip-hop, Malcom X in his youth sold weed to the Be-Boppers and was part of the cannabis cloud scene of Harlem by the 40's. Doesn't surprise me; just find it interesting how the cultures link in such a funny way. At 17, Malcom went by the name Detroit Red and sold reefers to the Jazz cats he looked up to. He told Alex Haley, "In every band, at least half the musicians smoked reefers, I'm not going to list names; I'd have to include some of those most prominent in popular music, even a number of them around today. In one case, every man in one of the bands, which is still famous, was on marijuana."

I can remember one day as a kid, I probably was around 9 or 10 years old. I was riding with pops in the white El Camino. "The Message" from Grandmaster Flash and the Furious 5 had come on WDKX the local black owned radio station. One of the things I was proud of Rochester for, was having a Black owned radio station. The D stood for Frederick Douglass, the K stood for King and the X stood for brother Malcom. All they played was soul and very contemporary R&B. They would play the occasional rap record, "The Message" being one of them. I was singing feverishly with the hook, "Don't push me cuz I'm close, to, the, eeeddddgggeee!" Pops turned the music down and asked me do I know what I'm singing. I had to think about it and said no, I just thought it was cool the way he was saying the words. Pops was like listen to the words, not the music. Comprehend what the man is talking about. "Broken glass everywhere, people pissin on the stairs, you know they just don't care," "Rats in the front room, roaches in the back, junkies the alley with the baseball bat" these are social conditions of the day he told me. "This isn't just a song, that's life," Pops told me. I never looked at that song or any other song in the same way ever again. I realized early, if your going to rap, you should have something to say. Other than that, you just rhyming, and Old McDonald can rhyme.

Throughout the sixties and seventies weed was synonymous with the hippy culture. Artists like Bob Dylan, The Doobie Brothers, and The Beatles and of course The Rolling Stones were all advocates of weed! For Hippies, rolling a joint, and passing it around in a ritualistic circle, was a way of affirming a community of purpose, however vague that purpose may have been. Weed was like the foundation of the psychedelic culture. Harry Shapiro put it best when he said, "If LSD was the icing on the counter-cultural cake, than marijuana was the basic ingredient."

Not that there weren't any Black Hippies, but my family wasn't really into the hippy thing. As many Blacks weren't. We were more on the side of the Black Panther movement. My grandparents had the velvet paintings in the living room of the African warriors and half naked Queen of Sheba. My parents had a traditional wedding, but my uncle Tony and Aunt Betty had an African wedding, they wore dashikis and all. I always looked back at those pictures and felt proud to be Black. Back then weed came in little yellow church donation envelopes. The envelopes were most prominent on Friday nights, payday! My aunt and uncle Tony and Tanya would come over with some more friends to kick it. My brother and I would be ushered off to our rooms, not to come out. My mom would reluctantly hang out. She was always a Church girl. On any given Fri day session, I would hear the likes of Stevie Wonder, Earth Wind & Fire, Marvin Gaye, James Brown and of course some Bob Marley. All of these artists smoked grass or pot as they called it at the time. Making subtle references within their classic records. But records like Stevie Wonder's "Too High" and Sly and the Family Stone "I Wanna Take You Higher" showed some artists could be a little more forth coming. Out of all the artists of that time, no one represented for the weed culture like Bob Marley. In the late 60's, in Jamaica the hottest thing going was The Wailers. At that time just as popular as The Beatles. Comprised of Neville "Bunny" Livingston, Peter Macintosh, and Robert Nesta "Bob" Marley, The Wailers dressed like gangstas or rudebwoys, wearing sharp suits and shades. Singing songs like "Simmer Down". After teaming up with producer Lee "Scratch" Perry and The Upsetters, Jamaica's premier session band, they developed the sound were most familiar with them having now.

Bob and the Wailers were the first to openly live the Rastafarian religion. Rastafarianism refers back to the Old Testament, identifying its adherents as the lost tribes of Israel, sold into slavery in Babylon and awaiting their return to Zion, the Promised Land. Rasta's characteristically grow dreadlocks, because a razor is never to touch the head of the righteous. Cannabis is the sacred herb, the healing of all nations. Cannabis has always played a role in the medicinal and mystical rituals of ancient Africa and was probably well known to the slaves who worked the West Indian sugar plantations.

These were the stimulants I grew up around. No particular artist or night with the family directly influenced me. To be honest, I was too young and can only remember the music playing while I sat in my room and played with my Hot Wheels race car set. This was way before video games, and I sure didn't have a TV in my room. We only had 1 TV in the house as it was. My father and I have in the past had a very tumultuous relationship. During the marriage and after the divorce my father had a problem prioritizing his family, like many young men. But now we constantly work at rebuilding our relationship. I love him to death as all sons love their fathers. I look just like him and as I heard from my mother all the time "you act just like your damn daddy!"

By the 80's my Mom, brother and I were back on our own. From time to time my Uncle Earl, my moms little brother, would come to hang in Rochester from Virginia. Earl is my late Grandmother's LucyMae's baby boy. Other than my Dad, he was the single most influential male in my life. He is a tall handsome brother with a dark chocolate complexion. He dressed in slick suits and had a pimps tongue. He taught me how to curse and use my size toward my advantage. Being a big broke kid in adolescence was awkward for me. I had self esteem issues. When my mom wouldn't buy those name brand sneakers, he would. For a kid getting picked on for wearing Bo Bos to school, that meant the world. Bobos were like the fake plastic sneakers you get out of the bin at K-Mart. When hanging out with him, he would play everything from Parliament Funkadelic to Alexander O'Neil. When Rick James made the all time weed anthem "Mary Jane", it was on steady rotation at Uncs spot. Those were the days of decadence and crack, and the music reflected it. Hip-hop being fairly new, it wasn't Uncs favorite. He had his peeps who he listened to, but Kool Moe Dee I would say was his fav. It was Moe Dees dress and voice command. Moe Dee used to be a member of the Treacherous 3, so he already had a Funk/R&B singer swag, so I got it.

Let me tell you a story about my uncle Earl. I think the year was around 1990. We had just moved back to the Va area to help with my Grandmother. Her health was starting to deteriorate and my mom needed another change of pace so we moved to Va. I had been brainwashed at the time that I wanted to go to Hampton in Va, and moving at that time would gain us in state status by the time of my high school graduation. Making my college tuition cheaper due to my residency. My uncle was always around. He was my encouragement while I played football. Helped me to stand up straight and push out my chest. At the age of 15, I was nearly his size. He would wear what he would call a "Player" suite. Basically the velour Gucci sweat suite of the time. He had several, of all different brands. I was often his sidekick. My Grandma figured, if he took me along with him, he had to bring me home at a certain time, in turn bringing him home at a safe time. See Unc liked to drink. Getting drunk and crashing cars was his thing. She constantly worried about him. This particular weekend, after getting paid, it was time to hit the town. Not sure exactly how I got to be the chosen wingman for the night, but trust I wasn't complaining. Any time away from the house I cherished. I honestly think he had compassion for me. I can't recall what particular event was taking place, but we went to Virginia Beach to hang out. My clothes were old and worn, so he allowed me to wear the Playboy track suite and he rocked the Sergio Valente. I felt like a star, you couldn't tell me nothing. He was the first person to give me that feeling. After that, I wanted it for myself. We hit the boardwalk, till the day winded down. We had dinner somewhere on the beach. After the meal, I recall the waitress telling Unc, hey we're closing the restaurant side, but if you want to continue drinking, you can hit the nightclub attached to the other side of the venue. Since you spent so much over here, I can comp you guys and have one of the security escort you over there. We get escorted into the club and over to a table pretty quickly. We were pretty much paraded in front of the whole club. We weren't the only Black people in the club, but let's just say we were like chocolate chips in milk. White women loooove my Uncle Earl, and of course he used to love em back! Right away women and male groupies bombarded us. It seemed as though everyone just assumed we were some big time football players. Two big black dudes, dressed in flossy track suits being escorted through the back door to the VIP, we looked special. My Uncle didn't persuade them otherwise. The people would come up and ask what team we played for, Unc would go "Come on man, I'm on vacation, I don't want to talk about the office" they would go "No prob buddy, what you drinking??" Within 30 mins, we had a table full of drinks and Unc was holding court with 3 fine chics, and the male groupies are in my ear by this time, since they couldn't get any with Unc. Now I'm having fun telling all kinds of extravagant made up stories for these Stan's, having a ball. By the end of the night, Unc tells his willing harem goodbye and were off. He's pretty toasted, but feel's he can handle the ride home. As we start to leave, I'm thinking how can I persuade him to let me drive. Lucky for us, it was late and there wasn't much traffic out. By the time we hit our exit, I suggested, in a very nice way, that maybe I should take over from here. Even though I had very limited experience and no valid credentials to be driving. But I figured, this was my chance since his judgment was a little impaired. In his inebriated mind he agrees, I hop in the drivers seat and we're off. We get almost all the way home and then I see the bright lights, here that siren, feel my stomach sink and my heart jump in my throat. Unc looks over to me and says, "Be cool!" The stout cop walks over to the car, "License and registration" in a deep southern drawl. "I don't have one sir" before the cop could even say anything, Unc goes off on me. Tearing me a new ass hole for what seamed like an hour to me. The cop felt so bad for me by the end of the tirade, he just let us go with a warning. When the cop left, Unc tells me it was all just an act. I was so convinced he was going to kill me, I wanted to go with the cop. By the time we got home, I was spent. Not only was I not used to staying up all night, but the night was insane. As a kid that was one of my most memorable nights, but it seemed like just another Sat night for Unc! He was a wild boy who's now a Pastor at a church in Va. I'm very proud of him for turning his life around and becoming a better person.

The parallels between my Dads love for Jazz and mine for Hip Hop doesn't seem to be by mistake. Many of the groups coming out in early rap sampled many jazz, funk, and R&B breaks. Cutting up the popular music of the time. Many a time I would be listening to a record and think to myself, I've heard that coming out of my pops speakers while kickin it at his crib. It's also no wonder to me why my Dad was a pot smoker, as they would say in his day. It was part of the culture. He may have not been a Black Panther, but he taught me Black Panther ideology. My family may not have been hippies, but I was definitely exposed to hippy culture through my Dad and Uncle. All I can say is, it's in my DNA.

Chapter 3
The Birth of BIG JAY

I started working with DJ's early in my career. I saw it as a way to get into the party for FREE. The first DJ I ever worked with was the homie DJ Big Reg. It had to be around '92/93 he and I was on the executive board of pretty much the Black Student Union at MCC. We was just kids, but he was already quickly becoming the hood favorite DJ from his street mix tapes and parties. One night he was like "I need a ride to this gig, help me carry my crates in and I would drink free all nite." Sounded like a bargain to me. I was probably going to go to the party anyway. Carry a crate and drink free, yes an actual milk crate, or we used the big square mail bins from the post office. They were slightly bigger than milk crates but with better handles. That way we can carry more records, lol. I had a great time, I told him let me know the next time he needed a ride; I would be down 4 sure! One night, there was a problem with the promoter as far as getting all his money that night. True homie status, I was making damn sure we wasn't leavin with out that bread. After the shenanigans, I asked Reg, "How come you don't have contracts, that's how you avoid the stupid shit." He told me, "if you wanna handle it, I'll cut you in on the bread" and BIG JAY ENTERTAINMENT was born, lol. I called the management company that because Puff had just come out with Bad Boy Entertainment, and I thought to myself, I want an entertainment company, whatever that is. The name of our crew was called HY-

TECH DJ CREW. We threw local parties around Rochester anywhere we could. I think our first party was in an abandoned warehouse on St. Paul over by Genesee Brewery. I think one of our homeless homies was living there. He said he didn't care if we threw a party so we did. Real Beat Street type shit. My homie Mando made the infamous HY TECH logo man and flyer design, and I was off to Kinkos! We was our own street team before the term was even coined, we passed them flyers out everywhere. The party was a smash! A real crazy night, if I recall the police came and turned it out on the early morning tip, so you know it went up!

I wasn't a weed smoker at the time. My crew wasn't into that, so I wasn't. We didn't do any other drugs either. But we did drink a whole hell of a lot. The music scene for us was filled with everything from disco break records that we would use for freestyle battles and such to grimy Brooklyn shit from MOP. Tribe and the whole Zulu nation resonated heavy with us. Dr. Dre had just dropped "The Chronic" along with the weed laced tales from Snoop Dog. Music shifted when he dropped that. Up until then, all the artists talking about weed where underground, Dre blew the lid off that. I believe he opened more doors for the likes of Redman, CoCo Brovaz and the Boot Camp Click; shout out to Dru Ha, the first white boy I ever saw tangled up in real rap. Before then rappers would have to shun weed on records. For a while rappers wouldn't even curse on a record, for fear of not being played on the radio. I remember when NWA and Eazy E dropped. It was like walking around with a nuclear bomb. If you got caught with that tape, TROUBLE. But even they wasn't talking about smoking weed much on wax. On "Express Yourself" Dre said that drugs would "Give a nigga brain damage, and brain damage on the mic don't manage."

Couple quick years later Dre drops The Chronic. I remember EPMD also had an ill verse toward mj. I can't blame em; it was the end of the 80's. Crack is wack! Was the slogan of the era. In the inner city ghettos, as they called em back then, crack rock was destroying our people. Some would argue if it weren't for crack there would be no Hip Hop. I am one who promotes this notion. By the 90's groups like De La Soul, Pharcyde, and Cypress Hill came out rappin about the Daisy Age promoting a much greener type of lifestyle. Coupled with Dr. Dre and the entire west coast movement, it didn't take much time before the weed leaf became Hip Hops national flower.

I met Green Lantern through Reg. He was already a familiar face in the Roc hip hop scene. He did production for some local artists. One that stuck out to me was The Roach. He was pretty much DMX before X. Just a grimy ass street dude. Green went to Brockport with another one of the homies Joe Sheez. Reg and Green started doing a weekly radio show on the college station, WITR, Rochester Institute of Technologies station. College radio was a big deal in the 90's for hip-hop. It's where many records were broke before going to commercial stations. It's also where real grimy underground rap could live because of the FCC rules. The shows would normally come on late Fri or Sat after midnight. You could pretty much do and say anything. This is where I would start to develop my professional relationships in music. Many of the radio reps at that time went on to become executives. If you didn't burn your bridge, you had a lane with a big executive like no other. When I first met Green Lantern he called himself DJ James 1. He was really a budding producer working with the local talent in the city, and he started DJing with our crew. This was great for me, now I have 2 DJ's to book out. When ones booked, I just booked the other.

After several years we had the city scene and the college scene locked in upstate NY.

Growing weary of the upstate party scene, I had my sites set on NYC. I knew that's where it was going to happen, if it was going to happen at all. By this time I had a girlfriend from New york and she was going home for the summer break. There was no way in hell I wasn't going with her. Her mother was an opera singer and caught a gig touring the summer over seas. This became the perfect opportunity for BIG JAY ENTERTAINMENT to establish some roots in the big city. My girl was from Harlem. At the time Mase and Cam were just starting to take over NYC and the entire rap industry with the Puff Daddy and BIG co sign. I wanted in any way I could fit in. I managed to get myself an internship at Jive records. I worked in the promotions department. We worked radio and retail. While in NY I would check in with the crew to find Green had started making mix tapes. Up until then Big Reg was the big mix tape king of the city. His blends were impeccable. Green having a background in production was able to add a lil extra something to the blends he would do. Using a 4-track machine, he would create blends with multiple instrumentals and insane intros like no other. He would give me his tapes and I would hustle them in the NYC mix tape scene as well as pass them around to record label heads, artists, people on the streets, anybody who would take em. Toronto also played a part in our come up. We moved a lot of tapes up there at Play de Record. A major part of the mixtape game that DJ Clue? made popular was having exclusives on your tape. Those days artists would only put out the best music on their albums, and most of the time you never heard all of the other music that was made. But from time to time a DJ would get their hands on a record that was supposed to end up on the cutting room floor, and instead it ends up on a mixtape for the hood to hear. This was around the time I started with the Fridge Magazine. The brainchild of Jonathan Levine, the Fridge was the documentation of the collision between urban culture and action sports. The first of it's kind. Now there's many hip-hop and action sports brands out there, but Jonny really had something special. By this time it's the late 90's early 2000's. I had managed to get myself fired from Jive, apparently my cute slightly older than me boss didn't like me calling her "Boo". I guess I had gotten to comfortable. It was my first time working at a record label. The atmosphere can be a little confusing if your not sure what your there for. The only other corporate experience I had was working a High School internship at Blue Cross and Blue Shield after class my senior year. Ties and proper language is what I knew. All the attributes of a regular corporate environment. At Jive, you could play music loud, curse and talk shit, and still have a job. It was the best. I took it for granite and learned a life lesson. Work is work, you play when you go home. So now that I was out of a job, it was time to find something else quick. Bills pile up quick in NYC; the cost of living is a little bit more than what I was used to. I remember answering an ad for a young marketer. I thought to myself, I'm a young marketer, so I applied and was called back for an interview pretty quickly. Upon agreeing to the interview, I though to myself, the address is on Madison ave across from the Sony building, it must be a prime position at record label, or marketing firm. I prayed all night for God to bless me with such a position. I met with Jonny the Fridges founder and CEO and Seth Zaplin, the magazines music manager. I recall it smelled like weed when I walked in the office, a shock for a job interview. It went well and I was hired immediately. I was the marketing and promotions guy, since I had experience in both. Jonny was pretty cool; if you can do it, make it happen. There was young talent in that office daily. Cool hip skaters and snowboarders to all kinds of rap and musical talent. The office was a true melting pot of cultures, talent, and races. He was really on to something. Looking back, I don't think any of us realize what we had at the time. Being a kid from sheltered Rochester I was meeting and conversing with all kinds of people from all over the world who shared in this common expression. A magazine is a common expression and collection of works from various people. The photographers, the writers, the editors, the graphic designers, there's many working parts. I got the opportunity to see this first hand. I also was able to develop some pretty good business relationships. Some I still have to this day. One of the common threads I saw with everybody was weed. It was the currency of our culture. Being in NYC where there are so many more people to police, it's a little easier to get away with smoking a doob in public. Not to mention most people in our culture smoked, so they would prob ask for a hit, before ratting you out. Smoking weed amongst the hip hop/skate culture of NYC seemed like a rite of passage. I've consecrated many a business relationship over a blunt. It was a way of developing trust. Almost like if we do this small illegal act together, we might as well have just stolen a car together. Needless to say, The Fridge is where I honed my weed obsession. Took my first hit from a bong at the Fridge office. I coughed all the way through it, and fell asleep 30 minutes after the hit, lol.

By this time, I was burning the candle at both ends on high

flame. My career with the Fridge was taking off to a great start, and Green Lantern had started to gain some buzz. Reg had a family, and it was a little more difficult for him to just take off on shows and promo gigs in the city, where Green would hop in the car and drive down to be with me any chance he got. He pretty much slept on my floor for years. I utilized every resource to get him more gigs, press opportunities, exclusive tracks and drops from the artist's themselves for the music. All while developing my own relationship with the artist's. A big supporter of the team, Rob Stone, who just started Cornerstone Promotions and was looking for the premier DJ to start his promotional mix tape series. He chose Green, which helped to open some national doors. The first big event I had to produce with the Fridge was an event called "Brooklyn, Vermont"; with this event we were taking the street hip-hop culture of Brooklyn and taking it to the snowy white mountains of Vermont. We booked Black Star, Mos Def and Talib Kweli, as the shows headliner early. We had a great relationship with Rawkus records, also run by Jews. Being able to network through the Jewish/Hip Hop community was effective when it came to getting things done. Next up was the supporting act. We wanted DJ Stretch Armstrong for his rap credibility and because he was white. We knew our audience very well, and wanted to make a great show the mostly white audience of Vermont could appreciate. Now the then radio promo guy at Interscope managed Stretch, Rene McClean, now turned big time record executive. He pushed a no name white rapper, produced by Dr. Dre, named EMINEM on us. He was foreign to us at the time, there was no music out other than a couple of freestyles, but that enough for him. On Seth's recommendation, we booked him. It was his last free show ever probably, lol. In a few short months, his name began to grow, by the time of the event in Jan 2000; his name was bigger than Black Star's at the time. We were ecstatic. While doing the show, I had a chance to meet Paul Rosenberg, Em's lawyer and manager. This relationship would prove to be fruitful a little later. We produced several Brookln, Vermont Festivals BK, VT. One year we had Fat Joe and Big Pun up to Vermont for the US Open of Snowboarding produced by Burton. Seeing Joe and Pun all smiles on the top of the snow was a great site. I can remember seeing Pun with his shirt off chilling in the dressing room smoking blunts, what a sight to see. He was every bit of 400+lbs and didn't care who saw it. Made me feel a lot more comfortable with my flab. RIP to the talented rapper. The next year we booked Gangstarr for BK, VT on another mountain in Vermont. We wore out our welcome at the first mountain, I always thought it was because we brought too many niggaz up there. Guru RIP and Premier was cool as shit. I'm still cool with Preem to this day. They smoked blunts with everybody, it was great to connect with them in that way. Legendary hip hop Presario Fab 5 Freddy was there just coolin and soakin it all in. The weekend was a huge party on a mountain. At some point I was in a lodge with a homie tryng to find a place to smoke a doobie. It didn't seem to be too much activity, but nonetheless we figured we should hit up the ladies room to smoke the doob. The logic was, if anybody walked bye and smelled weed, they would prob go in the men's room looking for the culprits. So we went into the ladies room, only to find Fab 5 and his homie, looking to do the same, with the same philosophy. Shocked that anybody else would think that way, we had a laugh and blazed our doobs in continuous rotation. I haven't seen Fab since that day, but can't wait to run into him and retell him the story.

Early in Green's career we had the opportunity to tour overseas quite a bit. This particular time we were going to Dubai for the first time and a couple dates in Germany. Giggin out of the country can be fun and exciting sometimes, but for the most part it is work, don't let em fool ya. Most of the time you're so tired from the entire traveling and strenuous schedule, you just want to sleep as soon as you get off the plane. If you're in a country where they speak no English, you can forget about watching TV.. Even at the 5 star hotels cable only had news in English. Which is cool, for a couple hrs., but then it's like, I NEEED VIDEO'S, lol. So let's just say, smuggling weed in our luggage became a routine practice. I would usually press the promoter to find it, since I had it placed on our rider. It was more of a test for the promotors. If they had the bud and hotels right, it usually meant they were on point. It usually meant they was connected in their town. Some would see it and be like, "Where the F*ck am I going to find some weed??" So I think the week prior, we had just come back from China, where we smuggled, and was good for the entire trip. Never having been to Dubai, I was unaware of the harsh drug laws there, but was soon to find out. We smuggled some weed as usual, and got on the plane. When we landed from the long ass trip, there was no luggage. I suddenly had that bad feeling in my stomach, but then to a sigh of relief, everyone's luggage was missing. We were told the luggage didn't make the connecting flight, and that all of the luggage would be there in the AM. So I was still kinda freakin out, due to the fact, we was still waiting on the records. No records, no show! So just imagine traveling with 4 big ass crates of records. We had to bring so much because you had to be prepared for anything on the road. Not to mention, Green's average set those days was, 2-4hrs. Green was basically raised by Big Reg, DJ Craig G & the Top Floor Crew, basically anybody he could get close to at the time to soak up any real party DJ skills. See party DJing paid the bills, and the mix tapes got him the producer recognition. The only other person who knew about the weed in the luggage was our road dog Noodles. There was usually no need to bother Green with minor details of how the weed got to the party. It was just my job to make sure it was there. Not to mention, by this time my weed habit had grown to a connoisseur status, and often when you're on the road, they have crappy weed. I'm not willing to take the chance. I'm thinking they wouldn't just hold up the entire flights luggage if they found the weed would, would they?? They do strange stuff overseas, so sometimes you got to wonder. But I went with the flow, they said everything would be there the next day, so I'm going to have faith. Of course, the promoter and myself get up bright and early and take the hour and half long trip back to the airport. We get there and only the records have come back. We're looking all over for the bags, but nowhere to be found. Now I'm starting to freak out. But I haven't had a shower in days, we have no clothes to change into, and the promoter is telling me the airport rep is telling him there are still more bags to be delivered. In my mind, I'm thinking we got the records, fuck the bags. We got away. By this time, I had already asked the promoter to get me some local bud, he almost turned White. He quickly informed me, possession of weed of any amount is a major crime, taken very seriously. So we leave the airport, do the show in Dubai in the same clothes. The party was on a Friday, when we arrived the entire city was in Church. Dubai is a Moslem city, which practices its religion on Fridays. We tried to go shopping but the mall was shut down. Even when it did open back up, the clothes were crazy old and outdated, it was better to just take a shower a put the same clothes back on. We were under the impression that we were getting our bags by the next city. We sleep, wake up and take the flight to the next city on the tour, somewhere in Germany. The promoter was from Germany, he swore his connections could get us our bags. I didn't want to let him know weed was involved until I absolutely had to let him know. Meanwhile I was paranoid as fuck checking in and going through customs for the next flight. In my mind, I'm thinking if they got the goods on us, they would've bagged us in customs, right?? But no, everything was smooth sailing. We get to our next city, still no bags, the concierge connects with the promoter. He goes "The airline is going to call me as soon they land" I'm thinking, yeah right! We get to the telly and get all checked in, and then I get a call from the promoter, with a different tone. Asking can he come to my room and speak with me, this is when I know the jig is up. He comes in with a confused look on face, asking me vague questions. Still unaware we had smuggled a fat ass ounce of stanky bud in our luggage, he says "The airline security called him and asked him to come down and claim the bags right away" But he said the guy had a funny tone about him, he had learned not to trust in that past when dealing with the German police. I had to tell him at that point what we had in our bags, and that was probably the reason the cop was asking all the funny questions. The promoter pretty much collapsed on the bed. I had never seen someone so scared. He said it's def better to get caught with weed in Germany than in Dubai, but it is still very illegal. So after I told him to take it on the chin, these are the things that happen when you book hip hop acts and DJ's. The plan was to finish up the tour and see what happens when we try to leave the country to go back. If we don't get stopped, were home free. The promoter said he would have to at some point turn himself in, due to the fact the cops had his info and address. He said, if he didn't they would be at his doorstep the next day. They don't play that shit in Deutschland. We went shopping in the small German town and ended rockin outdated Karl Kani for the rest of the tour. We finally made it home. Checking in and going through customs to come back had me shook like never before. I had never been that scared, just thinking to myself, if they nabbed us up there was nothing we could do. I called my lawyer before leaving, giving him a heads up, like if you don't here from us by tomorrow, come and get us, lol. The following week our booking agent contacted me saying that the promoter had to go to jail briefly behind our bullshit. I snickered arrogantly, "better him than me", why the fuck did I say that, I thought to myself. I was arrested the very next day in midtown Manhattan. Dam.

Chapter 4
Public Enemey #1

I truly believe in karma. I know in my heart I had it coming, especially after that dumb ass comment I had made to our agent. It was a regular business day in Gotham city. I started the day by getting 2 zips of some sticky ass sour diesel. My homie Spaghetti ran a delivery service and saw me as his first stop of the day. My usual M.O. was to have my street team guys hold down my truck while I ran in and out of the tall midtown buildings all day from one meeting to the next. Me and the crew were potheads, so waking and baking was the usual ritual. I was never stingy with my weed, if I had weed, they had weed! It was customary for the team to keep a blunt in rotation or at least a clip in the ashtray. Meetings can sometimes be long and stressful, so in between meetings, I would toke up. Shortly after my arrest I quickly stopped this practice. The day was ending and I was done with my last meeting. I hop back in my trucks cockpit and say peace to the crew. As they rendezvoused with the other guys to head back to the BX, I lit the clip they left for me and headed toward the tunnel. I swear I didn't get but 2 lights before I hear that NYC police make that beep sound like Ghostbusters , and there they were right behind me and I see the lights. Fuuuucccckkk! I quickly toss the blunt, roll the windows down and pray the jar of bud is in the stash box. As soon as the cop walks up he says "Damn, smells like a weed factory in there, license and registration buddy" He said he saw me light up at the light, which was odd to me because I had tints on my window. They run my license and I come back dirty. Now I'm getting asked to step out of the vehicle. Apparently in NYC when your license is suspended you can be arrested and do a night in jail. This was news to me and since I had never been arrested before, I was in total shock. I've had cuffs on me and been stopped and frisked but never arrested. They did a light search of the truck and allowed my crew to come and get it. So happy they didn't find that jar of sour, if they did this would be a totally different story. I'm quickly shackled to 7 other guys and mashed in to a patty wagon. Off we go to some midtown jail. I was booked and fingerprinted. I remember giving the camera an extra mean grill for the mug shot. Just in case the picture ever came up again, I wanted to make sure I looked mean and not scared. The first cell I was placed in was cold and dark. As I sat on the wood bench, all I could hear was jail noise. The guy in the cell to my right was babbling like a crazy guy, and in the cell to my left some guy going through withdrawal from some drug was going crazy. It's extremely difficult to focus. I close my eyes and pray. First thanking the big homie for allowing me to wake up that day. In my current circumstances I was still a lot better off than a lot of people, and I could never forget that. I just wanted to let him know that I heard him loud and clear. This was my big red stop sign. As I sat in my cell all I could do is think what would have happened if they found that weed. That much would have come with a felony charge. Had I not worked in the music industry, finding a regular job and passing a piss test might be a problem. I wouldn't be able to get a job. For the rest of my life I would have to check that box "Have you ever been convicted of a felony?" If I lived with my family in public housing, It would be illegal for me to return to my home. Healthcare benefits would be denied to me. In some states I wouldn't even be able to vote. These are just some examples of obstacles non-violent drug offenders would face. The court systems prey on the poor and uneducated. There are more Blacks under correctional control today than were slaves in 1850, a decade before the civil war. Since 1971 the war on drugs has cost over $1 trillion and resulted in more than 45 million arrests. The NYS Rockefeller drug laws were early in paving the way for the rest of the country in state minimums for non-violent drug convictions. I walked around my cell and read all of the graffiti from all over the world. I wish I had a marker to throw up my hood. I thought to myself, there weren't too many places I hadn't been in NYC at this point. As a kid who dreamed about living in NYC, I would've never thought it. After what seemed like hours to me, they shackled us again and we started moving. I was hoping we were on our way to see the judge and maybe getting released that night. Like on that TV show Night Court. But once they passed out McDonald hamburgers for dinner I knew we were there for the night. We were shuffled in cells by the two's, when they ran out of space, some cells got 3 people. My roomie and I were of the fortunate few to escape a 3rd person. I hit the cell first and sat down on the bench immediately. My roomie came in and rolled himself into a ball on the floor. Don't know if it was because I weighed 300+ or if he was just very tired, but I appreciated the lack of confrontation. Sitting hoping to fall asleep and wake up and it would be time to go, but all I could hear is more jail noise. I spoke to no one. There was no need for conversation. But it seems others couldn't help to tell everyone what got them busted or what they were going to do when they got out. One of the common denominators I could hear was drugs. Pills, weed, or coke seems to be the cornerstone of every arrest recipe. Another common denominator I recognized is that the majority of us were black or brown. Today millions of children in America have parents wrapped up in the penal system. Those children are more than likely to also end up behind bars. The war on drugs is more like the war on us with drugs. These charges create a viscous circle that perpetuates a functioning economy out of drugs, prostitution, and liquor in our inner cities. How do African Americans only make up 13% of the entire population of America but make up almost 90% of federal convictions for crack. Nixon first used the term "War on drugs" in the 60's. Most don't realize 2/3rds of his drug budget was dedicated to rehabilitation as supposed to enforcement. It wasn't until the election year did his priorities changed. During the 50's & 60's Jim Crow was in full effect. Post Jim Crow still had some lingering effects. As the predominately white hippies frolicked and experimented with drugs behind safe closed doors, blacks that experimented were subject to scrutiny. Over time the young black male has become the representative for all drug use in the media, and a target has been painted on our heads. Trayvon Martin and the many others who don't make it to the news are constant reminders of how screwed up our country is. I tossed and turned all night, who could sleep, I'm in jail. The guards woke us early in the am with McDonald breakfast. I thought to myself if they serve us Mickey Dees in jail, it's got to be crap. Back to the shackles. We were off to the courthouse. Now I'm in a gen pop type of cell with about 50 guys. Its white, with big thick windows. There's a bench that goes around the perimeter of the cell and its open in the middle. Here we got all kinds, bums, addicts, crazies, etc. I got to keep my guard up more so in here, you never know when you might have to knock a mufucka out. They finally call my name and I'm off to see the judge. Time served, I'm finally out!! I had the homies scoop me upon the same truck I was in when I got bagged. They never found my stash, so I kinda felt like I still won in some kind of crazy way.

PHOTO GALLERY

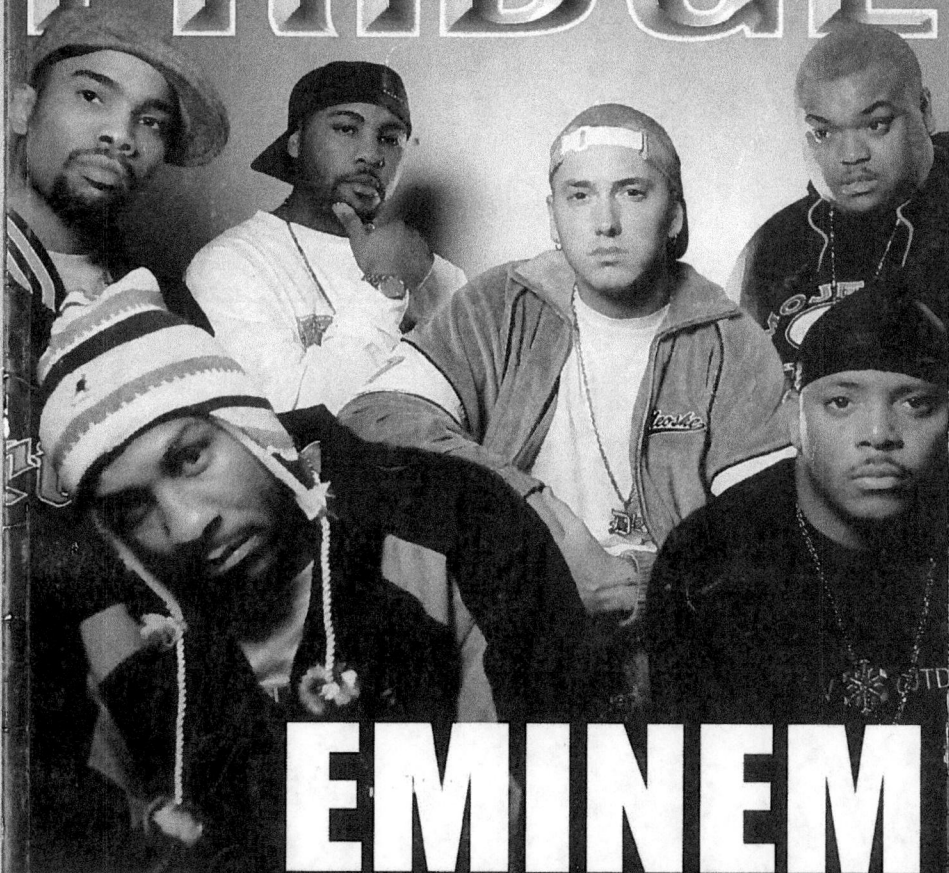

MUSIC SNOWBOARDING ART SKATEBOARDING URBAN STYLE

FRIDGE

EMINEM
& THE DAWNING OF D12

TREVOR ANDREW · THA LIKS · MARK APPLEYARD

ISSUE #00011   S/2001

USA $3.95   CAN $5.50

THE FRIDGE MAGAZINE PRESENTS
SUMMER SKOOL

NYC's ILLEST	PROFESSIONAL	LIVE
DJ'S	SKATEBOARD MINI-RAMP JAM	MC'S

BREAKDANCING - GRAFFITI - RECESS ROOM
NEW YORK CITY - AUG.11, 2001

NAME

AT speed nyc

FOR MORE INFO:
FRIDGE
MAGAZINE.COM

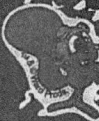

KLUB KUSH
DVD MAGAZINE VOL. 2
RAEKWON THE CHEF
K.R.E.A.M.
WARREN G
INVADES THE THC EXPOSE
KURUPT
420 DPG PARTY
DEVIN THE DUDE
SMOKIN OUT THE SMOKEOUT
THE ORIGINS OF
GRAND DADDY PURPLE
WITH KEN ESTES
Kush Kutie
BRITTANY COLOMBO
STRONG ARM STEADY · DJ GREEN LANTERN
B-REAL · XZIBIT · SCOOP DEVILLE
PARENTAL ADVISORY EXPLICIT LYRICS
"THE PREMIER URBAN LIFESTYLE GUIDE OF THE CANNABIS COMMUNITY"

Chapter 5
A Chronical History of Rap

Hip-hop and me were born in the same year. So I always felt like we were kindred spirits, whatever that means. Most of the kids in my neighborhood wanted to be pro athletes others wanted to be rappers, I wanted to be Russell Simmons. I wanted to be Rollin with Rush! He managed all of the hottest groups at the time. EPMD, Slick Rick, LL Cool J and more. Which was most of the Def Jam roster at the time. I respected the way he marketed and promoted all of his artists to be different. This was back in the day when record labels didn't put anything out but the best music. Whatever hit the cutting room floor never saw the light of day. These days everything is released, either on the album or on a mix tape. Russell passed the baton to others like Chris Lighty RIP, Puff, Dame, and Steve Rifkind who came in and innovated the game even more. The hip-hop industry wasn't the cash cow it is today. Many thought it would just be a fad and fade away. Hip-hop culture was born out of the hearts of inner city blacks and browns that just wanted a piece of the American dream. For so long we were denied and disregarded. Just like me, I guess that's why I relate so much to the culture. My kids listen to rap music, but they're more like that's my Dads music. I guess its how I can appreciate Jazz, but its definitely my Dads music. Hip-hop wasn't everywhere like it is now. Now commercials, TV show, and even the president acknowledges rappers and hip-hop culture. When I was a kid rap was confined to late night mix show on mainstream radio and it hadn't even hit TV yet. NYC had Ralph McDaniel's with Video Music Box. VMB would play all of the latest vids and have the freshest interviews. Then came Rap City & Yo MTV Raps, they were the only outlets for rap videos for a long time. We would congregate in little groups and exchange pause tapes with each other like they were books. Pause tapes were tapes that were made from recording music off the radio, pressing pause when the commercials come on. Waiting for the next song you like to come on and then press pause again to start recording. The first rappers I had ever met that were signed to a major label was Super Lover Cee and Casanova Rud. They had 2 songs out at the time, "Girls I got em locked" and "Do the James" both carried very heavy James Brown samples. This was early 80's, I had to be in middle school or maybe a freshman in High School. In NYC the City Kids Foundation decided to head upstate and put on a production and fundraiser. The City Kids Foundation empowered young people within urban communities with arts and educational programs. Exactly what we needed in the Roc. This is where I got my first taste of event production, something else I will have grown to love just as much as hip-hop. We produced a step show with talent from the local high schools and Cee & Rud performed. Since we were the shows producers we had a chance to kick it with them, take pictures and get autographs. I played the background much of the time and observed the whole scene. I guess it's the Scorpio in me. It was interesting to see the artist to management relationship; it seemed to me the manager was the one who was really in control. But as I grew within the industry, I learned it's more of a 50/50 cooperation, more like a marriage. I had a ball. I was so hyped to be behind the scenes making things work and seeing hip hop culture in full effect. This was also the first place I saw in person a real life hip-hop DJ actually DJing with turntables hip-hop style. Hip hop style meaning, turning the turntables sideways for easier scratching and flashing. I had the job of escorting him in to the building and getting him set up. I was impressed with the care in which he unpacked each piece of equipment and set up. The fact that the needles were kept in a separate case blew my mind. I didn't realize they were delicate and precious. After getting set up, he sound checked with a break beat I never heard before and commenced to flashing and chopping various breaks, I was hooked.

Still very much a shorty at the time, weed wasn't even in my vocabulary. Drugs hadn't really made an emergence within rap music just yet. The majority of the content still focused on girls, boom boxes, sneakers, basketball, real wholesome kind of stuff. Everybody who was rappin was kids. The older heads still listened to funk and slick R&B, hence the wardrobe of the early rappers. Feathers, boots and slick leathers. That was all reminiscent of that era. When Run-DMC hit, they wore what they wore on the block of Queens. Street niggas rappin on the radio. One of the earliest references to weed in a record is Run where he says in "Here we go" – "Cool chief rocka, I don't drink Vodka, but keep a bag of cheeba inside my locka" Even prior to that on Crash Crews "Ringing Bells" you don't here anyone rap about weed, but in the beginning of the record you here "Puff, puff up up and away" an obvious smoking weed references. Weed let alone drugs were hardly mentioned in rap records. Before Grandmaster Flash put out "The Message" drugs was pretty much absent. the message was supposed to be more of an anti drug song, but seems like it led to more popularity of cocaine to me. By 86' or 87' Scott La Rock, Krs-1 and Boogie Down Productions stepped onto the scene. They met in a group home in NYC. I gathered Scott was from Rochester. His name was Spanish for Scott from the Roc. In an early BDP song, "Superho" KRS mentions Rochester and shouts out WDKX, the local Black owned station. It was the first time I felt like the Roc was on the map. Due to that connection, BDP got steady bump in my radio. Hip-hop starting in the BX from the early influenced Jamaican park jams. So when KRS flowed "You see me step inside the jam with a spliff a sensei" you felt like you was there. KRS would produce a gangsta rapper named Just Ice who would make some dope references in his rhymes, but still tame compared to what N.W.A. did by 88'.

Eazy E and N.W.A. pioneered what we call Gangsta Rap today, rapping about drugs, sex, violence, police brutality, and racism with the angst of a whole generation. The first time I heard NWA it blew my mind. Summer break had just ended and a friend who had traveled to Cali over the Summer break came back to school with 2 tapes. Eazy E – Eazy Duz it and N.W.A. – Straight ought Compton. He had the entire school a buzz with this new music, which was heard to have cursing all the way through it. Not just one little curse word that they bleeped anyway. Cursing was still a big deal to us at that age. I begged him for days to bring his radio to my crib so I could dupe his tapes. This was before double cassette radios. To dupe a tape, he would bring his radio to my crib and play the tape loud on one radio while I recorded on my boom box. This would happen in real time, we sat there and listened to both tapes. I was in love all over again. I could never let my God fearing church going mother hear me listening to anything like this, I would be in trouble for sure. I was a latchkey child since a young kid, I was used to inviting my friends over and doing whatever I wanted between the hours of 2:20pm and 6:30pm when my mom got home.

N.W.A. member Dr. Dre went solo after Eazy's passing and produced "The Chronic", probably the single most influential record to the hip-hop industry when it comes to weed. After Ice Cube left the group and beef with Eazy E and Jerry Heller, N.W.A. wasn't as hard as they were in the past by denouncing drugs in the record "Express Yourself". Dre Stated "Can't see a brother smoking weed or sess, cuz it's due to cause a brother brain damage, and brain damage in the mic don't manage". By the time "Chronic" was released, the producer found a young pup named Snoop who he decided to pick up and let him ride shotgun. Snoops laid back flow tapped dance all over Dre's funk inspired bass loops making a marriage in hip-hop still together today. Solidifying the west coast win with Warren G, Nate Dogg and Tupac, Dre had a music powerhouse like no other. Not to mention, ushering in new lingo for weed in hip-hop that was only being used in Cali at the time. Dre and The Chronic opened the door, others like Cypress Hill, Redman & Method man, Gangstarr, and Biggie let the rest of the world into the party. Cypress Hill did for the Latino community just as much as Dre did for Black as far as influencing the young hip hoppers to smoke marijuana. In an interview I did with Cypress front man B-Real he told me Cypress rapped about blunts because the rappers in NY would rap about smoking blunts and smoking weed. Over the years I have developed a great relationship with B-Real and his crew. Over the years he has become a permanent fixture within the medical marijuana activist scene, always giving of himself to the community. One can't talk about weed and hip-hop without talking about the original southern smoker, Devin the Dude. Coming out of Texas, his laid-back swag and melodic flows about weed have always kept us in a trance. He was an obvious influence on the Swishahouse movement with DJ Mike Watts, Mike Jones, Slim Thug and Paul Wall. Swisha meaning all they smoked with were Swisha sweets blunts. Other Texas rappers who repped for the weed was the Underground Kings, Bun B & RIP Pimp C, UGK. You can see this in songs like "HI Life" and "In the morning". Another Texas artist who you might not think falls under the umbrella of hip-hop is Erykah Badu. She to me is one of the realest chics in the game. All of her kid's fathers are rappers, some would say by design. I just think she loves rap so much whom else would she be with. Her music continues to have weed undertones all throughout all of her projects.

Two rappers who blew the commercial doors off of hip hop for stoners are Redman & Method Man. With their movie "How High", countless commercials and TV shows they managed to be the high duo in the game. Appearing in the Def Jam documentary movie "The Show" you got a chance to see how there live show performance set stages a blaze across the country. Showing the well roundedness of there artistry. Still very impactful to this day, the 2 have release several solo albums and a few group album as well. I've had the opportunity to interview the Ticalion Stallion on his tour bus after a show. He told me about how much he loves his fans, and how much he trusts them.

Reppin for the Midwest, Bone Thugz n Harmony was discovered by one of N.W.A. founder's Eazy E. Signed to his Ruthless Records label, they went on to sell millions with his co sign and melodic choruses that the industry had never heard before. Ushering in a different rap style for that time in hip-hop. With songs like "Weed song" and "For bud smokers only" its no wonder Bone Thugz has the longevity it has today.

By the 90's and beyond most rappers dedicated whole songs to the topic of good kush, but most who smoke would drop subliminal and use the topic to make clever rhymes. Biggie was masterful when it came to this! I can say I met Big Poppa early in his career while doing a promo run for Dreams and Party and Bullshit. Of course my crew was DJing the event, who else was gonna hold down Big wile in the Roc. He was mad cool and humble, signed our copies of his 12 inch we had. Unfortunately I didn't have the opportunity to smoke with the homie, but memorable none the less. He wasn't even blown yet, but we knew he was the truth and was going to go far. Puff's name was out there, but Bad Boy just started and was puting all of their stock in Big and Craig Mack. He came back to town maybe a year or 2 later and of course he was the king of rap by that time. He had a show in town and my crew was doing the official after party at Club Babylon. He was just doing a walk thru and chill. He came and the club went bonkers. The most memorable thing about that night to me was when Reg played the Kwame record, Big got up and threw some water at the DJ booth yelling turn that bullshit off. It was a hot record that usually got the club crazy, but he wasn't having it that night. We totally forgot they had a little beef, but didn't think it was that serious. We quickly changed the record, nobody wanted to get on Bigs bad side. You cant talk about Big without talking about Tupac Shakur. In my opinion Big had him on the rhyming but Pac was just the realest. You can play some of his speeches today and they still have relevance. He was Thug Life to the day he died, and always kept it 100% with the hood. There's a story where he was driving in his car and witness what looked like some white boys harassing a black guy. He pulled out his gun and went to the black dudes rescue, shooting one of the undercover cops. What rapper you know today is going to go out of their way to help someone they don't even know in that way. I think he beat the case too. We miss you guys... Another connection to the Notorious one is the one and only Puff Daddy, aka P Diddy aka Sean Coombs. Green and I first developed a relationship with Puff around the time he was putting together the 2nd Biggie post humus album. He was looking for someone who could make music combing new artists with Bigs old accapellas. It was a dream to be working with Puff on the Big project. By this time he was going by Diddy. But similar to Russell Simmons, I had to call him Puff. That was the name he got at Howard University while being the best party promoter. I always heard they called him Puff because of all the weed he smoked back then. He wanted nothing less than perfection on the project. We were offered a room to work in at Daddy House, Puffs studio in midtown Manhattan. Green did most of his work in his home studio, but who could pass up the opportunity to work at Daddy's House. Who knew who you would run into, those vocal booths were legendary for the music made there. I had our usual Team Invasion crew there. We were brainstorming and going through the music, when Green and I were summoned to the studio next door by Puff. We walk in to see Swizz Beats and Busta Rhymes there with Puff and some beautiful women. One of them old school Bad Boy R&B dudes was there. I wanna say it was Rell, but it could've been Carl Thomas, can't remember. I do recall the homie Stevie J being there. This was soon after the Eve masturbation video had come out, and it was the first time I had seen him since. There was workers fetching food, blunts and smoke. There had to be at least 10 bottles of bottles of Moet there, the champaign was flowing and it seemed like a party. Puff was playing new music and wanted the homies opinion on it. The music was cool, and heads were nodding their heads. But

I can't remember anything particular about the songs. Busta was like these songs are dope, you mind if I play some music? Puff obliged him of course. The most ridiculous boom bap came out of those speakers. The whole room was blown away. Puff was so hyped from the tracks he was dancing on the tables and yelling "You got some shit!" He went from the table to the floor, and now he's dancing with the blunt in his hand and taking hits on beat. In my own inebriated state all I could see is Puff dancing with the blunt in slow motion. Thinking to myself, thats Puffy dancing right in front of me. I only usually see this on TV, I was blown away! After the soundclash, Puff and the entire room had to give it up to the winner, Busta! Not only did I smoke blunts and drank Moet with Puff and the crew, I got a dancing show too. There's been several sessions with Puff since then, but that was the most memorable by far.

Ludacris, Outkast, and 3 6 Mafia repped weed and hip hop for the ATL. I wish I had some cool stories to tell about doobin it up with Andre or Juicy J, but I don't. But I have had some interaction with Luda, but not a real session. He bought me some weed once, but we never smoked together. Another crew on my bucket list is Tribe and De La. Being a huge Native Tongue fan, I got so many questions. I've been to at least 100 shows over the years, but the only person that I've met and had a cool session with was DJ Maceo. Hanging out in grimy bars in the LES area in NYC is where I ran into dude. Just hanging out with his boys, soakin up some good rap music and vibes. Of course he was mad cool, but definitely a street dude. Not the flower child you saw in the videos. There's countless other groups in the rap diaspora that have a passion for the magical marijuana plant, but I'm keeping this about the more meaningful encounters.

Chapter 6
Smoking with the Gods

In all of my wildest dreams I would've never thought I would have made it this far in my career in music. Through my journeys in rap I've smoked with the best of them. After knowing Devin the Dude for a while I finally had the chance to interview the homie for Klub Kush. One of the questions I always ask is how old were you and what were the circumstances for your first time smoking the ganja. He told me a story about how he was with his brother on the playground. There was a guy smoking a joint on the football field. Devin told the guy, if you keep smoking that stuff you wont be good at sports, you wont be fast. The boy told Devin "I could beat you..." sure enough the boys raced and the boy beat Devin in a footrace hands down. After the race, Devin said "man let me hit that joint!" By far the funniest story I've heard on the topic.

Touring is the best way to meet and smoke with your favorite rap stars. Behind the walls of security where the tour buses align themselves is the land of label execs, publicity hounds, and your favorite rappers. After touring with Em on the Anger Management tour I had the opportunity to go on tour with the most notorious gangsta rapper of our time, 50 Cent and G-Unit. Shady Records and I had just started to negotiate terms for a deal for Green's mix tape album. I was offered a position in marketing at the label while the deal was going through. I truly believed in the back of my mind that

Paul just wanted to keep me around to make sure I wouldn't drift off and do a deal with another label. My responsibilities were very loose and not structured. I had learned my lesson from Jive about a loose work environment. I busted my ass to make a difference while I was there. I utilized my relationships to develop co branded promotional opportunities with Shady's artists. I also had tons of road experience, so it made sense for me to tour with the artists. As I was issued my bulletproof vest and given my schedule, you would think I would be scared. I loved hip-hop so much, I actually relished in the opportunity. See 50 was a phenomenal artist. By the time he was actually signed to Shady he was already being booked all over the country for shows, purely off his mix tape music alone. He was a beast! I had been around many artists before, but I have never seen anybody work so hard before. This was his 2nd chance at a rap career and there was no way he was being denied. He was an intense dude. The G-Unit crew would snap on each other all day as if we were kids in high school. Being from the hood, I was no stranger to the game. Being a big dude I usually had to keep a few jokes stored in my head on my surrounding crew. One never knew when the insults would fly, you just had to be ready or you would get fried. Imagine trading vulgar jabs with the guy who got shot 9 times and wears a bullet proof vest because he has people who are trying to kill him. I would always say something back, but I always tried to not be funnier than him, I didn't know him very well and didn't want to get punched in the face, because I outwitted the boss. The first time I met him, he kinda brushed me off like yea right this nigga's goin on tour with me. After finding out that Paul sent me directly, he labeled me the Shady snitch. I had to shake that moniker as quick as possible. In the rap community, the lowest thing you could be is a snitch. He figured since Paul sent me, my job was to tell everything that was going on, report back to the boss. It didn't help that I managed Green Lantern. At this time the mix tape scene was very competitive. An exclusive track from your favorite rapper could make you and your tape hot for an entire summer, as well as put good money in your pocket. This was still the age when bootleg cds and mix tapes were a very lucrative game. DJ Clue? made the game commercial and others like DJ Big Mike and Cutmaster Cee rose to prominence by following his blueprint, scavenging exclusives. Just to be the first to play the song on a tape, thus giving them the edge in the market. This was a real sport amongst the mix tape DJ's. I felt 50 never really trusted me for these reasons. Feeling this, I worked hard to gain his trust. He would always invite me to the gym to work out with him because I was a big guy, he wanted me to firm up my bulk. In hindsight I probably should have, but I was too busy getting high with Lloyd Banks & Sha Money. Smoking was limited on the bus, 50 didn't like smoke at all so we were limited to the times and areas we could smoke. But with 4 big time stoners on the bus, Sha, Banks, Young Buck who had just gotten down with G-Unit and was along for the ride and of course me, we found many ways to achieve elevation. We were usually confined to the back of the bus, which was set up like a lounge area. We would all bring something to the party and put the blunts in rotation. On the tour in addition to coordinating the retail promos and helping with the radio promo they would have to do, I would also go out and link with the local weed dealers in the area to get the stash for the night and following days until we got to the next major city to cop. Sweet job if you ask me.

Smoking weed is a favorite past time for artist on tour because of the hurry up to wait theory. Rappers are always late for shows, interviews, TV appearances, etc. The publicist or label rep always has the artist arrive hrs. earlier than the time they need to be there. Usually they are rushed there, just to wait in the dressing room for hrs. until they are needed. Thus, hurrying up to wait. During this time if you time it right, you could be in a cipher with some of the illest artists. While on the Anger Management tour I found myself smoking with the likes of Nate Dogg, Big Proof (RIP), Bizzare from D12, 2 Chainz & I-20 from DTP, Xzibit and many others daily. I would be remise if I didn't tell my Xzibit story. See the tour had just started, we were still on the east coast. Connecticut or Providence I think. I had a bit of a head cold so I decided to take a nap in our dressing room. I was the tour manager for the Eminem support group. My group consisted of Obie Trice, his manager and security, Dina Rae, the girl who sings background vocals on a lot of the early Eminem records, Shade 45's Lord Sear who played the ringmaster on the tour, Green Lantern and of course myself. It seems as though there was a production in process to catch backstage tour antics and pranks. I guess I was the first victim, because I was awakened to a face of freezing ice water. I felt like my heart had jumped out of my chest. I awoke to a camera in my face and all I could hear was the squeaky sound of wet sneakers running down the hallway. After cleaning up I went to investigate the culprit. After using the process of elimination I figured out it was Xzibit. I vowed to get him back, although this would be no small task. See X had a huge security guard who followed him everywhere, and I mean everywhere. I just knew I had to get him back some kind of way, but what could I do?? Now its weeks later and we're in Sacramento. This particular venue didn't have enough space for everyone to have a dressing room, so we had to share with Xzibit and his crew. I think we were at the Sacramento Kings arena. So the dressing room bathroom was set up like a gym bathroom, with open stalls. X goes "I'm bout to take a shit on you fools" because the area where we was chilling was in close proximity to the bathroom area. So we would be sure to smell his shit, if he took a dump. So as he goes into the stall I notice, his security is not around. I look over and I see that craft services had just dropped off all the food and beverages for the night. So there was fresh ice with the sodas. I quickly and quietly took the sodas out of the shallow reservoir and tossed the remaining icy water over the top of the bathroom stall. Icy cold water all over X, as he shat, then I ran like hell. I didn't care that there was no cameras there to catch my revenge. The people in that room know what happened, I know, and most importantly Xzibit knows. I returned to the area after about 45 minutes. I hoped things had cooled down by then. He was a great guy about it, dapped me up and gave me kudos for the sweet revenge. His big OG Blood security guard even gave me respect for the get back. For that day, I ruled the world.

There was always the occasional video shoot, but one that was kinda cool was when I had the opportunity to meet Quincy Jones. It was brief but memorable. Green produced a track for Ludacris called The #1 Spot using a Quincy Jones sample, Bosa Nova. We had the chance to meet him on the set of the video. Luda's manager Chaka Zulu hooked it up. He was a suave gentleman. He liked what Green had did to his music. He couldn't believe how the song sounded all chopped up. We chatted for just a few moments, he had to go to another engagement. I'm good friends with his son QDIII and had to name drop, hoping it would gain me some sort of cred with him.

When he left all I could think was that was the guy who made Michael Jackson's Thriller... Amazing! I know he worked with many artists from the jazz era to a bunch of new artists. But all I could think of was Thriller. Had he stayed a while longer, I sure would have asked him to toke up, just to see if I could pull it off, a brothas gotta try. This was also the first time I met the homie Big E. E came through serving some fiya! Luda copped a QP and tossed us an ounce. They didn't have a trailer for us, so we ended up smoking on the lot on the stoop of a trailer with no name. The plan was to rush the trailer after we made sure no-one was watching. Before we could even make our move, Lisa Raye comes out in all white as usual giving us the screw face. I guess she's not a fan of the ganja smoke, lol. Knowing I would be in LA from time to time, me and Big E would connect very often. I need that gas wherever I'm at.

Someone else who I didn't exactly smoke with, but I feel like the story needs to be told, is the time I met Beyonce. Now of course I'm a big Beyonce fan just like the rest of the world, but being a guy it's not exactly the music I ride around bangin in my car. Girl power doesn't compute to me. I get what she's sayin, but she's not talkin to me. After Green got himself fired from DJing with Em, we were fortunate to get him a job with the king Hov. This was around the time he had the shoe deal with Reebok. Green had chopped up some sounds of a tennis match to make a beat for the Reebok commercial. Hov rhymed over the track and it came out pretty dope! He had to come in the studio to change a part in a line and Guru had to mix it. Of course Green had the option to over see everything so we stopped by the studio for the session. We had heard from Guru that he might not show, but of course there was still work to be done. Meeting Jay-Z is always a pleasure. Up to this point I had interacted with him on several times and was used to being around him. Iceberg Slim is a very appropriate name, he's the coolest guy I ever met. His swag is infectious, he makes you want to be like him. He's his music in real life, not sure if that makes any sense, but if you met him, you would know. His homie OG Juan carries a very close swag, it's almost uncanny. This session was like all the rest, stanky ass weed clouds all in the air. Just as soon as we got the room sufficiently smoky, Jay-Z walks in with Beyonce. I swear my mouth dropped. I felt like I was in high school again and my crush walked in the classroom. I couldn't take my eyes off of her. Of course, I was tryn my best not to get caught looking. She was so beautiful I couldn't believe she was really there. Of course I knew they were together, but it didn't dawn on me that she would show up to the session. I felt embarrassed, I knew she didn't smoke, but the clouds did not offend her at all. Then I thought to myself, she's from the hood of H town, she's been around weed smoke before. She was kind and shook hands with everyone in the room. She even gave the young female intern a compliment on her shoes. She was a very cool and down to earth kind of girl. I felt like I was gonna get caught staring soon and would have to pay a fee for the amount of time I spent looking. She was so cool, I can't front I was envious of the boy Hov. After the meeting I called my wife and told her about the encounter. She wasn't too flattered of how I was crooning over some other woman. I had to tell her or else I felt like I was cheating, at least in my mind, lol.

Working with Green Lantern had its obvious monetary advantages, but getting the chance to work with some of my favorite rappers was a dream. All I ever aspired to growing up in Rochester, was to make the back of the Source in the paparazzi section. Back in the day The Source was the only magazine that covered hip-hop culture. On the very last page was the equivalent to TMZ today. It's where you might see a rapper at a party hanging out, our behind the scenes of a video shoot. Thinking I would be somebody's manager and be seen standing with my artist at the Grammy's or something. I grew up listening to the Leaders of the New School. I was and still very much a Native Tongue fan. There was nothing Tribe, De La, Gangstarr, or any of those dudes could put out that my crew and me wouldn't absorb in every way. I miss those days, I don't have the same feelings about rap like I used to. Of course the breakout star from L.O.N.S. is the homie Busta Rhymes. Busta is one of the most underrated artists in the game. Everything from his over the top dress and swag to his incomparable voice Busta can't be touched. All throughout the 90's he ruled the rap world and blazed every remix. Of course I knew every record and could quote every line. By the early 2000's he was in a funny place. He wasn't signed at the time and 50 Cent had NYC and the world going cray over doing mix tapes, so mix tape DJ's were in big demand. Especially Green, his presence on Hot 97, and Shade 45 in addition to the creativity he brought to the music there was no wonder we were able to reach the heights we did. The nature of most mix tapes had a real street tone, real grimy underground type of shit. Busta like many other artists would prepare exclusive freestyles for various DJ's they felt worthy or whom they had a relationship with. The bigger the DJ, the bigger the rap artist freestyle you had. It was a status thing that turned into DJ's becoming artists and dropping their own commercial albums on big labels. Within the Reggae culture they call em dub plates. In Reggae, you have various DJ crews that have been around for years. Stonelove is my favorite crew, me and the homies would listen to Stonelove mix tapes, drink Red Stripe beer and chew on chew sticks. We would talk in Jamaican accents and develop our Reggae DJ style. We started a sound crew called Fulfillment! I'm the selector Mista Burry, cuz I burry em dead! (In my Jamaican accent) and my homie Horatio Starr was the DJ. In Reggae crew the DJ talks on the mic and the selector plays the music. It was all in fun, we never played a gig but we da best!! After the crews got a bunch of dubs from the dancehall artists they fucked with they would battle with their dubs in a sound clash. I remember seeing Wyclef Jean battle in a clash in Jamaica where he played a Kenny Rodgers dub of the Gambler, mashed the crowd! Busta had a downtown loft close to Hot 97 so he would meet us right before we went up for the weekly show sometimes with a cd fresh from the lab. Sometimes he would tell us to stop by the pad after the show, seeing that his condo was right down the block, this became a frequent meeting. With the invention of pro tools you can make a real good sound quality mini studio out of a small space and that's exactly what he did. The rest of the loft had the usual contents, cool furniture and a huge flat screen. The other thing that literally took over 50% of the condo was his performance gear. He had tons of exclusive show outfits, furs, sneakers, and wild jewelry. Security was always a permanent fixture within the home in addition to Spliff Star. As a hip hop fan of course I was gitty as fuck! I would make sure I had the best weed to smoke out the dungeon dragon of rap. I always played it cool around artists, but most of the time I was screaming inside. Especially if it was someone like Busta, who I had grown up listening to. For this reason Green and I always gave him the upmost respect whenever dealing with him and his music. Busta also being a connoisseur would always have some loud with him. I would roll up, he would roll up, and Spliff would roll up. Next thing you know, the blunts never stop. There was always weed in rotation at Busta's house. We would be there for hours discussing everything from politics and the current state of hip-hop to the hottest video vixen. Music was always being played or recorded out of his little studio. It wasn't uncommon to see Rah Digga and other Flipmode fam there writing and recording. I swear Bust had a million songs. He's tried every style of rap flow and genre. Incredible songs I still haven't heard released to this day. He would play us different records and talk about his inspirations for the record, who the producer was, where the sample came from, all sorts of shit. I was like a crackhead at the carter, beam me up!! Just being around his inner sanctum, I felt honored. He had just had a bunch of legal issues with someone being killed at one of his video shoots, so he was very particular whom he let around. I remember we stopped by the spot shortly after he cut his long dreads. He saved his locks and showed Green and I. I felt pretty friendly at this point with him by now, this was like our 10th time there and 100 blunts in, we was fam in my eyes. I asked him if I could have a couple locks to add to a personal hip-hop museum I was curating for myself. I wanted to put them right next to the Christmas card I had gotten from Slick Rick, priceless shit! He politely turned me down, saying it was against his belief to let people have his hair. Something his Grandmother taught him. As I thought about it, my Grandmother taught me the same. She would always burn her excess hair from the comb or brush because she said if someone got a hold of it they could cast a spell on you. If Nana said it, it must be true, so I def couldn't argue with that!

All I got is 3 words for you, WU TANG CLAN. The Wu has to be the most influential rap group ever. What they have accomplished in hip hop, with their clothing, music business, and just being relevant for over 20 yrs. is no small feat. I've been there for the entire ride. I was stuck from the first time I heard "Wu Tang Clan ain't nuttin to fuck wit". That album and Tribes Low End Theory dropped on the same day, which was a great day in hip-hop. A bunch of hoodlums from Staten Island with a fetish for kung Fu movies. I was in my hood watching kung Fu movies every Saturday morning too. I could def relate to these guys. The way Rza would weave the kung Fu movie skits and samples in with the funky drummer and other soul samples was genius. Over the years I have smoked with pretty much the entire Wu Tang on one occasion or another. Except for Masta Killa. I even smoked with the late great ODB in his Roc a Fella days. Ghost and me would blaze up and discuss our diabetic issues, Gza was a staple at our Fridge magazine events, but I hadn't really toked with Raekwon until I got to Cali. A good friend of mine had a huge warehouse where he was growing massive amounts of high-grade ganja. So I would film interviews there all the time. I had the opportunity to bring Rae through and show him his first indoor grow. We did an interview where we discussed the philosophy of the Wu. How Rza always wanted each member to grow wings go out and pollinate the world. That's what helps the Wu Tang to stay relevant today. How weed and water is his staple, one of the many meanings of his label Ice H20 Records. Over time we shared many blunts and rap discussions. He even blessed me by hosting one of my early mix tapes K.R.E.A.M. Kush Rulez Everything Around Me! I also had the opportunity to smoke out and interview the homie Meth, The Ticalian Stallian. I caught up with him after the Smokers Club tour date in LA. It was a great show, the mix of Meth with Curren$y brought together a nice mix of old and young weed and hip hop heads. I hit the tour bus right before they pulled out. I forgot dude was that tall. I'm 6'2" and usually tower over most, but he had to be at least 6'5". Made me wonder if he had b-ball skills. Guess I should've asked him. Instead we talked about his first time toking up. He told me a story how he was around 16, and he was fronting with a blunt. Acting like he smoking, but not hitting it right. Someone saw him and called him out. The guy taught him how to do what he called an "Ooh La La Shotgun hit". A shotgun is when someone turns the font or blunt around in their mouth, fire side in the mouth. The other person puts their mouth near the other side and when the other person blows, its like a shotgun blast of smoke in the other persons mouth. The Ooh La La version came from the Sergio jeans logo from the 80's. The logo was a hand doing the OK sign. So what your supposed to do is use your hands as barriers, so you don't have your face or mouth to close to some other dudes face while doing the hit. I thought it was creative, some hood shit for the 80's. Another thing I realized while interviewing Wu members on the topic of weed, they all had responsible stances towards smoking and the kids. Stressing this is something for adults, and wanting to be very clear they was not endorsing smoking for minors and to always be responsible. Grown up rapper shit, I don't think they was talking like that 20 years ago.

To be most impactful within the rap music or any industry really you have to be very versatile. The more you can do the more you make yourself an asset, which makes it more difficult for them to fire you when you fuck up. Or when the pendulum doesn't swing in you direction. I forget exactly how I met Ice Cube. I spent a lot of time on the west coast spending time with my family while working, so I feel like I ran into him there. I do remember wanting the relationship and having to work for it. I can remember meeting him on the set of one his movies where I brought him some of Greens beats and mix tapes. We were in the middle of what looked like the dessert. He was doing a lot of action scenes and was dressed like a commando. He looked tired and not in the mood for much talking when I gave him the music. So I was surprised when he called back wanting to us to come by his studio session next time he was in NY. Watching Cube record was masterful. He was a real pro. A lot of rappers at the time would barely memorize their verses and then hit the mic to record, reading lyrics off the pad. Cube knew his verses before he even stepped in the booth. By the time he got to the mic it gave him the flexibility to change the inflection on his voice on different words, say some words different ways, it was masterful. He was so humble and cool. His road dawg WC was by his side with the Henny and weed like a real G. My whole crew was there. The opportunity to meet the legendary Ice Cube of N.W.A. was a treat for any real rap fan. They came in wanting pictures and autographs, they couldn't help themselves. Once again I couldn't believe I was experiencing this. I wanted to get as high as I could to properly enjoy the moment. He recorded 2 songs, one song was "Child Support" and another was a rap love song. It was weird to hear him rap like that, but like Busta he was trying other types of records. Ultimately he never released the love song, but it was great to hear him on a different vibe. I agree with his decision, I like my Ice Cube hard and not melting. It was a 2-day session. By the next day the euphoria had worn off and I was back to full time work mode. He had an album he had coming out and it seemed at least to me that his publicity crew had forgotten a major component of promotions. The hood dvd circuit. I immediately called the homie's Smack DVD and Frenchie aka French Montana who used to do the Coke Boys Dvd's back in the day came thru to interview the big homie. An Ice Cube interview for the streets was mandatory. On the hood Dvd's you could talk yo shit to the streets, you didn't have to be politically correct. This was before Worldstar and the social media boom, so mixtape DVD's was the only source for raw uncut hip hop, street fights, music videos and booty shakin. There was no need for proper lighting, most of the time they was just running and gunning for interviews so to actually get invited to interview somebody was great for them. He appreciated the love I showed him and has always been cool when I see him out. Being able to help him with his project warmed my heart. I always felt like I was part of an unsung coalition that made the hip-hop universe spin. We are the bearings on the wheels of rap world that makes it turn.

There are so many more stories to tell but I feel these are some of my most memorable moments of my professional toking career. I could tell you about the time Beenie Man kidnapped us in Jamaica to play his birthday concert, or how when Suge Knight first got stuck in a elevator with all of his goons at a Grammy party. Needless to say, no one wanted to be there when he got out. The party was cleared out by the time they got him out. But I digress.

Chapter 7
Ways we got high

Smoking weed out of blunts was and still is my favorite way to toke up. It's just something about the ritual of dismantling a blunt, breaking down some loud, stuffing it in the leaf, lighting the head and inhaling that first hit. Letting the smoke breathe through your nose, and blazing it till your eyes are fire red! My Dad smoked joints, so that didn't really appeal to me. I would see him smoking out of a bong, well it was more of a water pipe, pretty much the same thing. He called it a peace pipe, like the Indians used to use, lol. As a kid when I did smoke weed with the homies it was usually a bad grade of bud, so smoking out of a sweet Phillie Blunt was great. Phillie Blunts had become so popular it became fashionable to wear clothes emblazoned with their logo. By the time I moved to NYC everyone was smoking Dutch Masters. Guru, God bless the dead, from Gangstarr told us to use White Owls because they burn much slower. Once he said that, we jumped on that. As I got older it seemed the weed got better. I could remember just moving to NYC, after paying my rent and my bills on a Friday payday, all I would have left over is $20 for my entertainment budget. I would buy a $10 bag of bud, spend $5 on 2 bootleg movies, 2 DVD quality versions of movies that probable just came out in the theatres a week ago, to me was the one of the best deals goin. The last $5 was spent at the Chinese restaurant. Four wings and rice and a big ass ice tea was enough food to last me the night. The rest of the weekend I would find some chick to feed and fuck me. I was so good I could stretch that dime in to 3 blunts. By the time I started working at the Fridge, we would smoke weed during our marketing meetings, it was a great environment. There was always weed around. The art of rolling good blunts and joints is an art form. Those who have perfected it will be quick to display their skills for you. Rolling a blunt is like a weed ritual you like to do for your friends, one that I take much pride in performing. It all starts with a fresh cigar or Backwoods. You don't want stale, dry ass leaf, it will fuck up your entire smoking experience. I actually still prefer using the mini Dutchies. I like the leaf on the cigar. Phillies and wraps are more of a homogenized leaf like material. The dreads use Fanta leaf, for that real natural taste. I like to use Backwoods from time to time too. In Oakland Mac Dre RIP used Backwoods, because he said they were the most expensive. Next you need some good quality bud broken up to small crumbles. One good gram of some OG or some good kush will always do you good. Some will say you need to stuff the blunt like a cannon with over 3 grams, not necessary for a good experience. But if you got it and it's a party, stuff five of them. In my opinion, I don't like to break it up to fine, you can get a dusty blunt, who wants that. Break it up to small to fine crumbles. It should be sticky, have a moist feel and smell great. Roll the bud nice and tight. Loose pockets of air create the canoe effect when burning. You don't want to use too much moisture when securing the leaf. Allow the air to dry, I know a lot of people will use the lighter to flame dry the blunt. But a natural dry provides a smoother burn. Sometimes while lighter drying, you can burn small holes in the blunt. Before lighting do a dry hit on the blunt. It should taste great and have a sweet bouquet in your mouth. Once you light the spliff, make sure to take 2 puffs and pass. Gangstarr made a whole song with instructions. After you puff, be sure to pass the dutchie pon de left hand side so the blunt can move in a clockwise rotation. Musical Youth taught us that. Reset and do again, until sleep or the munchies sets in. Now during the smoking of the blunt there may be a few things you might want to watch out for. Understand, your getting high, so there might be a few things that might miss you. Usually it's not a big deal, other that something to harass your friends about while smoking. Someone in the cipher might get a little talkative and might need to be reminded to smoke or get off the pot. Pun intended. Something else that is very common with a triangle cipher is the ping-pong effect. While smoking and talking, your talkative 2 partners might start to pass the blunt back and forth between the 2 of themselves. So you might have to step in or you will be sitting there not high, while your 2 friends are blazed out of their minds. Other than somebody jumping out of turn in the cypher, that's all you pretty much got to worry about. In my travels I found that the taste in blunt is very regional. Dutch Masters are usually an east coast, NY thing. I first heard of Swisha Sweets from Swisha House in Houston, but I know the west coast prefers the Swisha too. Papers have made a strong comeback. I have grown to like using papers. Due to the great bud in California, I really want to taste the weed. Using a glass piece or good papers is usually the best way to taste good weed. People who also smoke quite frequently say the cigar paper is too much like smoking cigarettes and to harsh. Artist's like Wiz Khalifa, Rick Ross, Action Bronson, 2 Chainz, B.OB. and Curren$y have been carrying the baton for the culture. Of course there's many more, but these are definitely the most prominent. They probably feel like I did as a kid with the mindset of, my Dad smoked blunts, I wanna smoke joints with my good ass weed! Of this rap generation, Wiz has definitely become the poster child for weed. But I don't feel the stigma is what it used to be. People don't care like they used to. Not quite sure why people started using blunts, I can only assume it was for camouflage and to mask the taste of bad weed. If you're in an area where smoking is still illegal, you have to be very careful where you blaze up. It's very difficult to try and convince a cop you were smoking a cigarette, when he can plainly see from afar the difference between a joint and a cigarette. But it might be easier with a blunt to say your smoking a special cigar. This is the same reason why vape pens have become so popular these days. Especially in non-legal areas, vape pens can be confused for a regular writing or e pen. Vaporizing weed gives off vapor and not smoke, making it difficult to detect if you're in a crowded club or public place.

Smoking with glass has become a new favorite. I didn't even smoke with a bong until I got to the Fridge Magazine. Generally Blacks tend to stay away from glass, it reminds them too much of smoking crack. Not to mention the possession of a bong is considered paraphernalia and could be used for probable cause and an inspection. One needs to be smart, especially if you're Black, a stoner, and live in an illegal state. After speaking with all of my White and Jewish friends, they all had bongs. They hid them in their rooms while in high school. I would've never tried anything like that. Living with a Black mom is like living with a private detective. She would come in my room and inspect every so often trying to catch me with something I wasn't supposed to have. All she would find is porn. The first time I hit the bong it was a long day in the office and we were hangin out after hours, which had the likely hood of turning into a party most nights. Drinks would flow, friends from the industry would drop bye and of course the weed would be flowing! Bongs and pipes were a staple in the Fridge office. This particular day, I guess we were out of blunts and I was encouraged to hit the bong. After a quick lesson, I was ready! Of course I coughed up lung the first time, but after that I quickly mastered it. After a few bowls, I was sleep within 20 minutes, out for the count. Somewhere there are pictures of me hunched over my desk, drooling on some paperwork. Using the bong will make you a lot higher per hit. As the water cleans the smoke, it's possible to get more smoke in your lungs allowing more THC for the brain. When first learning it's a tricky dance with the carb, which can be a slide or just a hole. You need to learn when to inhale as well. Clearing the tube is the rush, and holding the massive amount of smoke in your head, can feel like your gonna bust, if you don't know how to breathe while hitting the bong. The glass industry has grown into it's own industry and become a major part of the glass art culture. The detail on some of these glass pipes is insane, and it get's crazier and crazier everyday. People's imaginations are turnt up when it comes to creating functioning art for smoking. The technology has grown immensely too. Different ways of cutting the glass to create chambers that can catch the ash, coils that you freeze to make the smoke colder, all sorts of crazy shit. Bongs have become pretty run of the mill for today's smokers. Bongs are probably the most used method of smoking in TV and movies. The bubbling sound of someone hitting a bong is pretty much the signature sound for smoking. Followed by the slivering inhale of a joint or blunt, sounding familiarly like a snake. The old jazz crews in New Orleans back in the 30's were called the vipers, due to the sound they made while hitting the joint. Dabbers also use bongs fitted with special nails that resist high heat. Dabbing is reserved for the experienced toker. Instead of a bowl, the nail is usually heated by a blowtorch. Only a blowtorch can produce the right amount of fire to heat the nail to the temperature needed to burn the concentrates. Dabbing and vaping oils have become the new wave of getting high. I personally am much more a fan of the flowers. Once you start breaking down the plant material to a wax or shatter form, the THC levels are way more concentrated, hence the term. There seems to be great debate on what's better, concentrates or flowers. I feel it's more of a lifestyle choice.

Last on the list are edibles. Edibles can be fun. They have more of a pill effect, once it's in your body you can't shake the buzz. The edible game has expanded to new levels. Now there's cannabis infused sodas, chocolates, tinctures, candy and all kinds of food. The art of cooking with cannabis has stepped up quite a bit too. There's all kinds of recipes for everything from gummy bears to gourmet desserts and savory dishes. My experience with edibles is make sure you eat them on an empty stomach. When you have a full belly, they don't seem to work as well. I thought for a long time that they didn't work, until one day I had a bunch of cannabis cookies. After smoking and having the munchies I tore into them. I knew they were medicated, but I didn't care, they were good and tasty. About an hour later, I was stuck on stupid and couldn't stop laughing no matter what I tried. I couldn't come down off my high. The reason why I'm not a big fan of them. When smoking a blunt or any other method, when you start to feel you're self-getting too high you just put the weed out. I don't like to be taken on rides I don't agree to.

Chapter 8
The Future of Weed is Black

After years of working with Green and host of other DJ's and rappers, the scene was starting to get a little old. My twins were born in early 2000. My wife and I tried to maintain a family in dirty Jerz but it wasn't exactly clicking right. I was constantly on the road away from her and the boys. Early on it was very difficult for her to try and work and be the mother she wanted to be. Not to mention she's a Cali girl. She like's to wear sandals and pretty dresses; the snow wasn't working for her. Not to mention the music industry seemed to be taking a turn. Artists weren't getting the types of deals they used to get in the past, labels had to figure out a different way to generate revenue, the old business model was no longer relevant, with digital distribution taking over. Not to mention the NY rap scene was slowly turning into Atlanta. Since raps inception NYC has always held a strong hold on the scene. Of course other regions have gotten a chance to rock, most notable the west coast. But since early 2000's the South has worn the crown. Ever since, NY rappers have been struggling to find their sound. I feel it's never left; NY rappers have to embrace themselves. I was over it, time to move to LA. My boys were growing up and needed their Dad in their lives 24/7. I grew tired of having to visit them in between gigs and business for a couple weeks and to have to see their faces when it was time to leave. It would break my heart whenever i had to travel and be away from family. It got worse as they got older and was cognoscente of time. They would ask me "Daddy when you coming back, I would say on the 15th, they would say, Geez that's in 3 weeks" sounded like forever when they said it like that. Not exactly having my pops around all the time growing up, I felt a necessary desire to be in their lives. Not exactly knowing what I what I was getting myself into, I left NY and moved to LA for permanent residency. Green and I decided to part ways. Our visions had become conflicted. He was lazy and very much an artist. Very self conscious of his work. He wouldn't want to put anything out unless he felt it was perfect. I love the music, but it was all about making money and progressing for me. Whenever I wanted to sign other DJ's to work under him, his concern was that they would be better than him. I told him that's what we want, so we can eat off them. Who wants to keep working for the rest of their lives. I had some savings, so I figured with my relationships and my hustla mentality I could pretty much keep doing what I was doing from more of an independent perspective. Marrying corporate entities with artists, tours, events, etc. looked promising in a lucrative LA market. No one told me the recession was going to hit. Everybody was suddenly wiped out! It was like a bad storm had just hit the world. Anybody who was writing checks in the past, stopped! Anybody who was hiring stopped. All of my money wells started drying up quick. The industry was already fickle, when the recession hit, everybody changed their numbers and ran for the hills. For fear someone might try and take what little coins they had. Shit got cray! So what did I have to do, turn to the streets. Fortunate enough for me, there's a medical marijuana movement in California. I was probably here for a year before I had even heard of a medical marijuana clinic. My first visit inside one, I lost my mind. I didn't even know there was that many kinds of weed, I didn't even know there was a difference. In NY there was Thai bud, Sour Diesel and Reggie, short for regular weed. Once I was getting money all I ever smoked was top shelf. I had to be educated on the difference between Indicas and Sativas. I picked up a couple of the medical marijuana trade magazines on my way out. Once home all I could do is smoke my high-grade medical marijuana while I flipped through page after page of advertisements and stories of medical marijuana patients. I couldn't believe how many clinics, products, and patients were involved with medical cannabis. As I sat high as hell, all I could see was a vision of me as a kush entrepreneur. I thought to myself, as long as I was smoking weed, I had never ever seen an urban counterpart to High Times. That's what I always envisioned Klub Kush to be. But I wanted to add an educational element. I wanted people of color to understand why this plant is illegal in the first place, and to understand the box society is trying to put us in. I feel cannabis is the next movement we should own. For years they have used it to enslave us, why shouldn't we use it to liberate us as a race. We already got the advertisement sewn up. Everything we rap about in our music sells 10x over. Just ask Nike, Timbaland, Polo, Ciroc, and the list goes on and on. Wiz alone has sold more weed to the collective community just by rapping about it.

Harry Anslinger, the Director of the Bureau of Narcotics from the 30's once said "There are 100,000 total marijuana smokers in the US, and most are Negroes, Hispanics, Filipinos, and entertainers. Their satanic music, jazz, and swing, result from marijuana use. This marijuana causes white women to seek sexual relations with Negroes, entertainers, and any others." He might as well have added rap music to that list, because I've never seen any other form of music make

White women want to have sex with Negroes. In our country, people of color have always been targeted for drugs. Even when it has been statistically proven Whites use more drugs. In June of 2013 the ACLU put out a report called "The War on Marijuana in Black & White" Billions of dollars wasted on racially biased arrests. Our country has wasted huge amounts of money just to systematically keep the Black man down. Back in the Jim Crow south, it was the law for Negroes to have separate but unequal conditions. They used the color of our skin to discriminate against us. Once that was outlawed, they had to switch up the rules to the game. Over time the Black man has been labeled as a problem in society using fear. It's manifested when young men like Trayvon Martin, Mike Brown, Eric Garner and many others are murdered. Making it OK to do away with our lives, deeming us not equal. It's not what they say is the law, but in how they treat us, actions speak louder than words. By locking us up in absorbent numbers and making us dependent upon an illegal functioning economy, there is an obvious chain of destruction for the poor and uneducated. I often wonder if Whites fear that we will one day rise up and enslave them.

The media for years has portrayed Black males as savages. In the movies, TV, and the news we have been identified as a problem to society. Fear is the tool used to manipulate the masses into making it OK to kill off the poor. But nowadays Whites are just as poor and are starting to complain about the conditions. They call it the Occupy movement. Once a group has been singled out and determined to be no good, it's easier to exterminate them. If no one cares, no one will come to save you. The quote that Anslinger made singles out Blacks and other musicians of color as the problem for loose White women. Was that the biggest fear of White men at the time, that they were sexually inferior to Black men?? Or did they fear a tan society, instead of Black & White?? A melting pot of all races cultures is what I see for the future.

Next comes ostracism, when you establish one set of rules for one set of people and a different set of rules for another group of people. New York recently reformed their Rockefeller drug laws, which mandated harsh mandatory minimum prison terms for simple, low-level drug offenses. Under these laws, people convicted of first or second time low-level drug offenses receive long prison terms -- not the treatment or support services they often need. They also recently deemed the long time practice of stopping & frisking unconstitutional. These are laws that have been in effect for decades. Locking up millions of poor young men of color, all the while keeping the jail systems running. Michelle Alexander talks about it in her book, The New Jim Crow. We are forced into low-income housing. Banks won't allow loans to people with felonies. If your family needs a loan for a house you get denied. If you were an entrepreneur looking for a loan, you were denied. Drugs effected families of color in all kinds of ways. You don't have to be the one doing the drugs to be effected. Your family could be the receiver of a death due to violence produced from drug activity. These are things that can impact a family for generations. It's no wonder many Blacks had very little to nothing to do with any kind of drugs, for fear the little rights given to them might also be stripped. As we enter into a new time where marijuana legalization is on the horizon, more people of color should be involved within the industry. It's forecasted to be a Billion dollar industry and the people of color are already being blocked out. The industry is becoming white washed with the term Medical marijuana. With Colorado, Washington, Las Vegas and now

California going legal, the media puts White faces with the medical cannabis scene, but then associates Black people with the illegal side of it. I'm here to tell you there is no difference. Medical & street weed is all the same. Every time I see these medical shows advocating marijuana there's only Whites represented on all the shows. A Black woman could never sign on to be a Mom for Marijuana; for fear of having Child Protective Services come in and have another reason to disrupt the family.

Which leads to confiscation, the next level in the chain of destruction. Poor people are losing their rights and civil liberties. When you can't afford proper legal representation, a stop & frisk could mean real jail time for you. The majority of the people getting ushered in and out of the court systems are poor people of color. When you are denied health care, decent housing, your constitutional rights it opens the door for your property to be seized and then you know who's next to go…

Where we live plays more of a role in the quality of your life than you may think. Simple everyday things like the cost of gas and fresh vegetables in your local grocery store deviate from area to area. They don't allow liquor stores and fast food chains on every corner in the suburbs. But that's the kind of crap you see laced in the hood. Resources are limited, not many people are there to network with to get out of your situation. Hip-hop was born out of these conditions. We have single handedly turned an underground phenomenon into a multi-billion dollar industry recognized worldwide, a very similar story to the cannabis industry. Through our music and culture we have made marijuana the most popular it has ever been. For us not to share in the profits of the industry is ridiculous, especially since we've already paid so much. People of color need to bum rush the weed industry like it's the mall and Jordan's are on sale. It's the last remaining industry yet to be capitalized by the government. In a sense, now they are coming for one of the only sustainable industries we had in the hood. Once the local weed dealer is off the streets, and the cash flow doesn't go back into the hood, someone's not going to eat.

When people don't eat people die. Annihilation, the final step in the chain of destruction. Back during Jim Crow days you would just be hung from a tree in your front yard. Nowadays they just shoot you for being in the wrong neighborhood at the wrong time. Weather its direct or indirect, the people who are paying the price are the young people of color. We still have more fighting to do as a collective culture. The herb brings all races, creeds, and cultures together for one high! That's why I'll always be married to marijuana!

Chapter 9
Ghostface

Speaking of Wu-Tang, I have to tell you about my recent Ghostface story. Now I've met Starks in the past while recording Green Lantern's album. We did a song called "Trials of Life" featuring Prodigy from Mobb, the soul crooner Bilal, and of course Tone. Prodigy rapped about his sickle cell, and Ghost rhymed about having Diabetes. Having had the sugar disease myself we kicked it all nite about how the disease effected us personally and the tribes of having it. A classic hip hop moment for me! Anytime I got the opportunity to converse with a rapper a respected, I felt that much closer to the culture. For some reason, I also felt that nights like that somewhat made me more of an exec in the industry. I know many people who work at the labels in many positions who never get a chance to talk to their favorite rappers, let alone have a meaningful conversation. So when I got this last minute call from Tones manager, who's a good friend of mine, to DJ for him at a party in Vegas. He said his regular DJ and backup was previously booked and that it was cheaper to fly me from LA than some random DJ from NY. I was thrilled! But very scared at the the same time. I have DJed many parties and played music for many a rappers, but nobody on this caliber. I wanted to prepare in every way tomato sure I was on point. I stressed a sound check, if I had that, I knew I would be cool. I was told the show music would be emailed to me any minute. When I say last minute, I mean I got the call to do his the day before the show. I had already made plans with a good friend who birthday it was. I make sure I got all of the necessary tools needed to DJ on a guest set. My needles, slip mats, Serato cd, headphones, etc. Making sure everything was in top working order. I patiently wait for the music, so I can go over everything. It's no problem when it's a Ghost song, but what about when he wants to do a Wu song? Does he just do his verses, or does he do the whole Wu song in those situations? I've gone to individual Wu-Tang member shows, and I've seen them do whole Wu songs in their sets. Knowing that I'm dealing with hip hop timing, I tried to be as patient as possible. Of course, I don't get the music until I'm sitting in my hotel room around 8pm. Of course I'm freaking out on the inside, because, not only did the music come dumb late, but theres no soundcheck. I'm not even sure why it didn't happen. Me and the manager was already in the process of getting instrumentals off the internet for a plan B. Even when the music came, all of the songs wasn't present. So now I'm in Tones suite trying to get a few minutes to go over the music for the night. The only people in this beautiful top floor Vegas suite are me, Val the the manager, Wu-Tang's Killa Priest, the promotor, a guy and his Latina girlfriend with her boobs popping out all over her dress. I wondered if they were there for the big blunts of OG dude was rollin up of was it for the big titties in the room. I didn't mind either by the way. Of course Tone was there holding court. Meeting him this time was like meeting him for the first time all over again. I didn't expect him to remember our Diabetes conversation, this is a guy who probably meets at least 50-100 new people every week. I thought he might remember the song. Most rappers tend to remember their music. I felt I might ask him about it given the chance. But now didn't seem like the right time to ask about the music. I put it in the hands of the manager. Technically that's his job, to interact with the artist and get things done. So as any good manager would do he stepped in and got us together. But even then he was preoccupied with something. He told me to come back after he takes a shower and get ready, then he would be ready to finish going over the music. I begrudgingly agreed and waited. Now the set time is 1am, it is now 12, the promotor is starting to igg the manager, but of course is on his own schedule. I am also patiently waiting, having been on the other side with the artist for so many years, it felt funny to see it from this perspective. Of course when Ghost comes out ready to go it's pretty much time to start heading to the venue. Usually the artist would stay at the same hotel near where the club is, but for some reason Tone wanted to stay in his favorite suite in the Palms. The party was at Light Nightclub in the

Mandalay Bay. That's where me and everybody else was staying. I thought of it as a production flaw, but who knows the exact reason why he stayed there. I was caught up in my own inner hell. Not only did we not do a sound check, but I have yet to go over the set list with Tony for the show. I am literally walking around behind him as we enter the sprinter to go the the venue with my laptop open in my hand discussing songs, and cue points. As he's giving me instructions, I am frantically trying to type notes into my phone. All while I'm trying to decipher his Wubonics. Now we're in the hotel walking thru the huge lobby finding our way toward the club. All while Tone giving dap to the fellas and hugs to the ladies as we walk thru the huge hotel hotel tunnels lined with slot machines and high end retail stores. Finally we get the backstage area, it's well after 1am. The Henny is flowing and the blunts are in rotation. Surprisingly Ghost didnt't smoke this particular day. Of course, I was after the opportunity to smoke and chill with dude creating another memory to put in my hip hop files. But none the less, there was enough going on for this story. So now its me, the manager, Priest, the promotor, and now the clubs owner, some asian dude who I think is doing tees with Tone, and of course some random thots. Me and Ghost are still trying to finalize this set list. As he gets a bit self conscious, he kicks everybody out of the room. Said he felt like everybody was looking at him, while we was going over the show. I appreciated it, I felt the same way, but didn't want to say anything, it wasn't my show. I have done many a hip hop show and knew anything could happen on stage. He told me just watch my hand for the signal to go to the next song. So we finally finish the set list, and then I hear "You ready??" Uh I think so, but in my mind, I'm not so sure. I am wisked away to the stage. There was a DJ already on the set, there was a combination of turntables and CDJ digital turntables. The soundman asked me how many turntables would I need. I promptly replied 4. Did I forget to mention on another note, I could only hear in one ear. I had just had ear surgery and I was recovering with some sort of antibiotic gel in my ear causing my temporary hearing loss in one ear. My left ear, the ear I usually use while DJing. I can hear ear, so I wasn't totally useless for the night. Me being left handed I cued up the first record on the left table. The sound man pointed at the table to my right. Eluding that that was the turntable my right record will cue up on. I was in such a nervous stumper I just went with what he said. The promotor was in a rush to get the show going, it was already 1:30 I'm sure. Everybody was looking at me, like LET"S GOOO!!! I was ready to get the crowd hyped on some DJ shit, getting the crowd to chant Wu-Tang and yell for Tony Starks. But before I could look, Priest took my microphone, and ran to the stage. In the back of my mind, I was sorta relieved. So I drop the first record, everything fine so far. I go to load up the second record on the right platter. For some reason the song doesn't load up to the appropriate

CDJ. I'm looking on the other CDJ's trying to find the record so I could assign the mixer to right channel. But I couldn't find it, as the seconds are rolling by in what seemed like slow motion to me, The set starts with Criminology and after the first verse right in to Ice cream. Of course I missed the first cue because I could never find where the other record loaded up to. The music stops, now I'm getting mean mugs from Ghost, because I messed up the first cue. Now I'm only working with one turntable the entire show. The sound man is no where to be found. I'm drowning live in front of the Light nightclub crowd. I end up doing the rest of the show with very choppy and haphazard. I took the cake when I played the Cher Chez La Ghost instrumental, and it didn't have the vocals with the girl singing. It was the only instrumental I could find online. The regular DJ didn't send that record in the email. Tone just walked off the stage, I was heartbroken. I felt like dog shit. I just fucked up this mans show. I know this guy to be a real street dude, so I as soon as I collect my headphones and other belongings, I make a b line right for Ghost. I'm copping all kinds of pleas. I didn't want any kind of beef with dude. Lucky for me he had already gotten paid and now had some titties in his face to pre occupy him. By this time we are now back in the backstage VIP area, and all I can see all over his face was how bad the show was. I'm not sure what to do… I want to go to my room, and beat my head against the wall for failing my love hip hop and Ghostface. But I'm no punk, and I wasn't gonna run from any confrontation. But at the same time I wanted to express to Ghost, how sorry I was. After he had a chance to calm down and process the night, he told me if the universe swayed it in that direction, there was nothing any of us could have done about it. But trust, it was the underlying discussion all night. Around 5am in the Vegas diner Peppermill, we talked about it man to man and chalked it up to a learning experience. I felt like DJ Enuff in that classic video where he fucks up Biggies music on a MTV taping. I could def relate. I knew if he could bounce back and have a career, I knew I could do the same and keep mine. On a lighter note, I knew that Tone would never forget me now. I'm sure if I see him 10 yrs later, and I bring up that night he will def remember. I didn't smoke with the god, and I fucked up his show. Every story is not going to have a rosy ending when your talking about my life. I'm just glad I didn't the fresh off the block Tony Starks. I might've had to knuckle up catch a fade with him, which wouldv'e also been just as memorable. I don't think I will be getting that call to DJ with him any time soon.

END

www.ingramcontent.com/pod-product-compliance
Lightning Source LLC
LaVergne TN
LVHW052034080426
835513LV00018B/2311